A PARIS CHRISTMAS

FOR SALE

A PARIS CHRISTMAS

BY JOHN BAXTER

Previously published in the UK in 2011
with the title *Cooking for Claudine*

First published in the US by Harper Collins in 2010

Previously published in the UK in 2011 by Short Books
with the title *Cooking for Claudine*

This edition published in 2015 by
Short Books
Unit 316, Screenworks
22 Highbury Grove
London N5 2ER

10 9 8 7 6 5 4 3 2 1

A CIP catalogue record for this book is available from the British Library.

All interior images courtesy of the author's collection.

ISBN 978-1-78072-247-4

Printed in Great Britain by CPI Group (UK) Ltd, Croydon, CR0 4YY

Cover illustration by Vince McIndoe
Cover layout by Rose Cooper

Also by John Baxter

For my French family

Contents

Contents

Preface

I was preparing dinner with the help of my friend, the Movie Star.

"When you first meet people," I said, "do they ask you when you first knew you wanted to be an actor?"

"Not very often." He wiped his hands on one of my aprons. "Where do you keep the English mustard?"

"Fridge door," I said. "Don't you think that's odd?"

He dumped a teaspoon of canary-yellow Colman's into the paste of soft butter, flour and black pepper, and began to cream them together.

"Not really. I'm not sure I could tell them anyway. I think you're born with it—like being able to waggle your ears."

"And yet people always ask me when I first decided I wanted to cook."

"Oh, well, yes; they ask me that too. All the time.

They see me making a soufflé or boning a chicken, and they say, 'Where did you learn that?' As if it was something unnatural ..." With a soft spatula, he started to smear the butter and mustard mixture onto the *côte de boeuf* we'd be eating for dinner that evening. It creates a crust that keeps the juices in and makes the beef particularly succulent. "Who can remember, anyway?"

I can.

I was five; maybe six. Our family was spending two weeks at a tiny seaside resort on the Australian coast called Wottamolla, south of Sydney. It's in the middle of a national park, so there are almost no houses today, and there were even fewer then. Our hillside shack was mostly verandah. We could see the only store in town from the front door, which is why I was given a metal billycan with a wire handle and a tight lid, and told to walk down and buy two pints of milk.

When I hadn't returned in an hour, my father went looking—and found me sitting on the beach. I'd taken the lid off the can and was carefully trickling handfuls of white sand into the milk.

The Movie Star stopped massaging the last of the paste into the beef.

"And this taught you what about cooking, exactly?"

I remembered how the grains glittered as they flowed from my hand, and the way the milk snuffed out that brilliance. The sand looked so light, it surely must dissolve, I thought to myself. Yet when I stirred the milk with a stick, I could feel the drag. The sand hadn't melted. It was still there, a sludge at the bottom of the can.

"It taught me that sand might look like sugar or salt," I said, "but it didn't act the same."

"You don't say. Before you uncork any more revelations, let's get this in."

We skewered the beef with the rod of the rotisserie and slotted it in place in the centre of the oven, which was already up to 450 degrees. I closed the door, reduced the heat to 175 degrees, and set the timer. With a stately motion, the beef began to turn. Sex, drugs and rock and roll are all fine in their way, but give me a good oven every time.

"Even at five," my friend said, "I knew sand from sugar. It's only actresses who are dumb."

Well, of course I knew the difference too. I just didn't know why they were different, and what that difference meant in practice.

"That must be why you're the movie star," I said, "and I'm just a common scribbler."

"Must be." He topped up our glasses from the bottle of Château Lafitte Rothschild. Nice to think that part of his salary for the last piece of TV tripe was being spent in a good cause.

"So... you discovered sand wouldn't dissolve in milk," he said. "What then?"

"Oh, that was when it started to be fun."

From understanding why sand was not sugar, and sugar not salt, it was a short step to butter and oil, and why foods acted and tasted differently if you cooked them in one or the other, or a combination of the two; why egg whites made things light and yolks made them heavy; why it was important to know whether to put the salt in at the beginning or at the end; why you never used chicken skin in making stock, why chopped garlic tasted different to crushed, and why, in baking an apple, you never cut out the whole core... the important things, that make the difference between food that is just edible and something that feeds not only the body but the soul.

So you see the capacity to cook will see you across more frontiers, make you more friends, give you more pure satisfaction, win you more admiration—even love —than any language or skill. Food can provide solace, it can sustain, it can satisfy and seduce. I had arrived in France as a foreigner not speaking a word of the language, and within a few weeks, without ever having had a cooking lesson in my life, found myself preparing Christmas dinner for twenty members of my new French family in an eighteenth-century château in the presence of my formidable mother-in-law, Madame Claudine.

How did this happen?

Well, pour yourself a glass—because it's a long story.

1

A Good Tooth

I've noticed that people who know
how to eat are never idiots.

—GUILLAUME APOLLINAIRE

When our daughter was eight, Marie-Dominique and I overheard her talking to another child as they bounced on a trampoline at a beach in southern France.

"Je suis une petite australienne," Louise explained, *"et mon papa est cuisinier."*—"I'm a little Australian, and my father is a cook."

Neither statement was quite true, nor quite false either. Louise does hold dual Australian and French citizenship. And I do cook our meals, and have done so ever since I moved to Paris eighteen years ago to marry her mother. And each Christmas, for some years, I've

7

also prepared Christmas dinner for my adoptive French family, up to twenty people.

In hell, it's been said, the drivers are Italian and the police French, while the lovers and, worse, the cooks are English. The Australia of my childhood still thought of itself as an outpost of the British Empire, and ate accordingly. Scandalously for a country abounding in succulent fish and seafood, fresh greens and salads, in mangos, papayas, and pineapples, Australian cuisine comprised hot dogs and meat pies, fried fish and chips, overcooked roasts, soggy vegetables, and canned fruit with canned cream. Meals were less a case of "chips with everything" than "chips *instead* of everything".

I can see most of my life as a flight from the horrors of the Australian table. It's ironic that, almost as soon as I left for Europe in 1969, its food began to improve, until today there are few countries where one can eat and drink so variously and well. But by then it was too late. I was launched on a voyage that would take me, via the cuisine of a score of cultures, to safe harbour in the gastronomical capital of the world, and cooking Christmas dinner in Paris.

That a person raised in rural New South Wales, in the heart of the meat-pie-and-peas country, should end up preparing Christmas dinner for a French family with roots deep in the soil of medieval France, and, moreover, do so in a country house dating from before Australia was even discovered, seems the height of improbability.

First, I had no training as a cook, no experience in a restaurant, no *diplôme* from the Cordon Bleu school of culinary art. What I knew about food I'd learned the hard way, as a means of survival and to satisfy a craving to taste interesting things. Some people are born with a knack for drawing, the ability to sing in tune, or that flair for theatricality Noël Coward called "a talent to amuse". My inborn talent was more selfish. In Australia, anyone possessing a healthy appetite is said to have "a good tooth", and my qualifications for this title were impeccable.

Second, I was not French—a fact my new in-laws felt as keenly as I did, but were ready to endure because I made Marie-Dominique happy and because, far more important, we had added a child to the family.

My third deficiency was social. How could I become integrated into a distinguished French dynasty when my forebears were so low class? Specifically, the Australian branch of the Baxters was descended from a criminal, albeit a not very skilful one. In the early nineteenth century, my English great-great-great-grandmother stole a bucket and was transported to the penal colony of Botany Bay, never to return. (She was one of the lucky ones. Had there been anything in the bucket, they'd have hanged her.)

As it turned out, I was wrong to worry that Marie-Dominique's family would think less of me for my convict forebears. The French are no strangers to vice. Indeed, they invented many of the more interesting ones and have worked hard for centuries to perfect the rest. To the French, sin—provided it is conceived with imagination and carried off with flair—is like the dust on an old bottle of burgundy, the streaks of grey in the hair of a loved one, the gleam of long, loving use on the mahogany of an ancient cabinet. It's evidence of endurance, of survival, of life.

2

Stranger in a Strange Land

A fine dinner should be a ceremony,
an evening's entertainment.

—JULIAN STREET

A Christmas dinner was the first event I attended in France as a member of what would shortly be my French family. It was the winter of 1989 and I'd only been in Europe for two weeks.

Struck down by that helpless love which the French call *un coup de foudre*—a thunderclap—I'd abandoned a comfortable life in Los Angeles and, on the spur of the moment, moved to Paris to be with the woman I loved. That I should relocate so suddenly and completely seemed lunatic to my Californian friends—even more so since I knew no more French than one can pick up from movie subtitles.

A week later, as I brooded in Marie-Dominique's tiny studio apartment on the Île de la Cité, in the heart of Paris, staring out at this grey European city swept by a freezing wind straight off the steppes of Russia, I could almost agree with them. Was I out of my mind?

What kept me from getting the next plane back was my lack of a good overcoat.

If my cultural and linguistic skills were unequal to France, my wardrobe was worse. In Los Angeles, we adapted to winter by switching from short-sleeved shirts to long, and on really cold nights—when the temperature dropped to the sixties Fahrenheit, say—draping a scarf around our necks.

On my first Sunday in Paris, I made the mistake of accompanying Marie-Do on a walk with no more insulation than a sweater under my jacket. After I'd turned an ominous shade of blue, we took refuge in a café thick with cigarette smoke—mixed, I was later to discover, with the microbes of that virulent bug the French call *la grippe*. It put me in bed for a week. By the time I felt well enough to flee back to California, it was too late. Christmas had arrived.

That Christmas Eve, in the late afternoon, we drove west out of Paris, following a sun that was already, at four p.m., sinking below the horizon. Speeding through the leafless forest of the Bois de Boulogne, we followed the *périphérique* along the Seine, then swung across the river at Saint-Cloud, and headed for Versailles. Fifty kilometres beyond was the village of Richebourg, and Christmas dinner in the country home of Marie-Do's formidable mother, a retired university professor, long-widowed, whom I would learn, in time, to address as Claudine.

Once we turned off the highway into a maze of country B-roads, the France through which we drove was one in which the three musketeers would have felt completely at home. Farmhouses of brick, hulking and two-storied, squatted amid vast unfenced fields, their ploughed soil dark and rich as chocolate. Geese in the barnyards hooted indignantly as we passed.

Every few kilometres, a high stone wall and a carefully tended wood behind it announced the presence of a château. From the road, we glimpsed only the tall wrought-iron gates, a gravelled drive, a façade of pale grey stone, chill as a glacier.

The country home of Claudine—she also kept an apartment in Paris's sixth arrondissement, overlooking the Luxembourg Gardens—proved less daunting than these stately homes, but only just. I stared in awe at the stone fireplace, large enough to lie down in. The gnarled, toffee-coloured chestnut beams, held together with wooden pegs rather than nails, still bore the marks of the adzes with which the carpenters, now more than two centuries dead, had shaped them.

Through the floor-to-ceiling windows, the garden, dotted with old peach and cherry trees, sloped away under a sky pricked with stars. In my state of mind, no landscape could have looked more desolate.

I loitered around the living room, clutching a glass of something sweet and alcoholic that might have been sherry but wasn't. Around me bustled the preparations for a French Christmas dinner—activities in which I was supremely useless. I examined paintings or watched flames devour the logs in the fire. Occasionally, I circled the dinner table cluttered with crystal, porcelain, and silver, and counted again the fourteen chairs, wondering which would be my particular hot seat.

Periodically, a car drew up, and cries from the kitchen announced the arrival of more relatives. Dutifully, Marie-Do brought them to meet me. The first, her *tante* Françoise, a commanding woman who was also her *marraine*—godmother—regarded me from over her spectacles and politely wished me *"Bonne fête"*.

Each new arrival brought something for the feast. Françoise's contribution was a bowl of chocolate mousse, thick and dark as the soil we'd seen in the ploughed fields on our way here.

"Riche," I suggested.

Françoise raised her eyebrows and turned down the corners of her mouth. *"Ce n'est pas . . ."* Remembering I was a foreigner, she shifted into her limited English. I was to get to know this effect—rather like a marathon runner who's been pelting along on concrete suddenly slogging through deep sand.

"It is . . . hmph hmph . . . not so rich, I think. Just . . . rph hmph . . . the cream, the *chocolat*, some . . . er, cognac, and . . . hmph . . . *comment ça se dit* . . ." She muttered through numbers, one of the hardest things to learn in any language. *"Un, deux, trois . . . vingt-cinq . . .* umph, twenty-five eggs?"

Jean-Marie, Marie-Do's brother-in-law, could hardly have been more different in style. He arrived on a Harley, with Marie-Do's sister Caroline on the pillion. From the worn leathers and the grease under his fingernails, I'd have taken him for a mechanic who'd married out of his class. In fact, he was a highly placed civil servant, while Caroline ran the Paris campus of a major American university.

Jean-Marie offered a hand as thick and rough as an oven mitt. *"Bonne fête."*

"Er . . . *bonne fête* . . . um . . . *aussi."*

He peered into my drink.

"Ah, le pineau de Charente." He sorted through his limited English vocabulary. "You like?"

A. CHAZELLE.

"It's OK. I was wondering what it's made of."

He looked blank. I fell back, as I was increasingly forced to do, on sign language, dipping a finger, tasting, miming a query.

"*Oh. Il y a du cognac, et . . .*" But mime could only go so far—where was Marcel Marceau when you needed him?—and I had to buttonhole Marie-Do to translate his motions of squeezing . . . crushing . . .

"It's brandy," she explained, "mixed with fermented grape juice, crushed from the skins and seeds after they've made the wine. You like it?"

Like Françoise, Jean-Marie had brought something for the dinner. Wandering into the kitchen, I watched him remove it from the pannier of his bike. Unwrapping half an issue of *France Soir*, he revealed a large glass preserving jar. Inside, immersed in golden fat and looking like the organ of a very ill alcoholic, was an entire goose liver.

As carefully as a surgeon handling a beating heart, he slid it from the jar onto a board.

"*Cuillère,*" he demanded.

Someone handed him a spoon. He scraped off the fat—to be reserved for the creation of baked potatoes, crunchy golden on the outside, meltingly tender within.

"*Torchon.*" A cloth completed the cleaning.

"*Couteau.*"

Decades of use had weathered the knife's handle almost white and worn the blade razor-thin. Judiciously, Jean-Marie sliced the liver into slightly more generous portions than one would receive in even the best restaurant—a demonstration that this was "family".

He'd just finished, and the women were arranging the slices artistically on a dish, flanked by the small, crunchy, pickled cucumbers called cornichons, when Françoise returned. Following her was an imposing white-haired man in his early seventies, dressed in a double-breasted blue suit, silk tie, and white shirt—her husband, and, as I'd been warned by Marie-Do, the famously reticent and moody alpha male of the family, Jean-Paul.

An eminent scholar and scientist, Jean-Paul had retired from a highly profitable career as an analytical chemist to become a painter, at which he achieved even greater success. François Mitterand, president of the republic, twice chose one of his paintings for his personal Christmas card—the sort of accolade that really counted with the status-conscious French.

To me, he accorded a gloomy *"Bonsoir, Monsieur"* and a limp handshake, before disappearing into the dining room. From the doorway, I watched him put on his glasses to examine the labels on the night's bottles of wine, lined up to breathe on the stone mantel above the open fire.

With Jean-Paul present, the meal could begin. A few

minutes later, he took his place at the head of the table, and the other dozen guests arranged themselves, with me at the foot.

The marathon of Christmas dinner commenced.

I'd been warned what to expect. After the foie gras, we'd be enjoying white *boudin* veal sausage with fried apple, then roast *pintade*—or guinea fowl—a *gratin dauphinois* of sliced potatoes baked with cheese and cream, accompanied by green beans and carrots, followed by salad, cheese, and Françoise's twenty-five-egg mousse— each course with its wine, including champagne with the dessert.

The goose liver was delicious enough for one to spare little thought for the poor bird that produced it. We smeared it onto fresh white *pain*, larger brother of the more familiar baguette, washing it down with '84 Bordeaux from *Madame*'s own *cave*—which was literally a cave, hollowed out of the rock on which this house was built.

The women never stopped handing around plates, offering more foie gras, and returning to the kitchen for bread or cornichons. Jean-Paul exchanged a few phlegmatic words with Jean-Marie, then fell silent. From time to time, he would tilt a wine bottle away from him and stare at the label, as if it might have changed miraculously into a better year.

I began to see the problem.

I was the problem.

Marie-Do had gone to Los Angeles on vacation and returned with this . . . person.

Who was I?

Seducer, fortune-hunter, boyfriend, bigamist? Was I there for the weekend, the month, or should I be regarded as a permanent fixture? If so, would I be an ornament to this tight little clan or an embarrassment, to be hushed up and apologised for, like cousin Nicolas, who, as Marie-Do had explained, periodically broke with his girl, wrecked his apartment, climbed onto the roof, and had to be locked up for his own safety?

I was at this supper for only one reason—to sing for it. But what could I tell these people which might convince them I deserved their hospitality, let alone their friendship, even their love?

Without quite knowing what I was about to say, I cleared my throat. Conversation halted. Every face turned in my direction.

"In Australia," I announced, "I had a friend . . ."

3

George

*...and I thought of Jack ... looking just like these men,
hard and strong and confident and with brown legs planted
in the Seymour dust as if the whole world was his to conquer,
a man fulfilled in his own rightness ...*

—GEORGE JOHNSTON

My friend was a writer. His name was George
Johnston, and when I met him in 1964, he had just returned to Australia after decades spent in China as a war
correspondent and in London and the Greek Islands as
a journalist and novelist. *My Brother Jack*, the first in his
trilogy of autobiographical novels, had been a bestseller,
and was about to be turned into a TV mini-series—as
good a reason as any for him to come home.

George and his wife, Charmian Clift, trailed the

titillating perfume of their wild reputation. Who in Australia's literary world didn't have a George-and-Charmian story? Their drinking, their fights, their infidelities—all were legendary, and this return to Australia merely magnified them.

I got to know the couple when I included one of George's stories, about their life on the Greek island of Hydra, in an anthology I was editing. To me, they were figures out of myth. Charmian embodied the aging Circe, still able to enchant us with the raddled shreds of her beauty and the remains of an aristocratic drawl, now roughened by decades of booze and sex.

As for George, rail-thin and already having lost one lung to tuberculosis, nobody gave him long to live. Yet he spun tales tirelessly, of navigating the mountains of China with the Flying Tigers and sampling the bohemian decadence of peacetime Greece. He punctuated each sentence with a drag on a sodden cigarette, and paragraphs with a phlegm-flecked cough. Listening to him talk, I understood the old sailor of whom Coleridge wrote in his *Rime of the Ancient Mariner*, who spellbinds a young man with his tale:

He holds him with his skinny hand.
"There was a ship," quoth he . . .

George was never more hypnotic than when he described how, the war over and their future uncertain, he and Charmian shivered in the fog-shrouded London winter of 1947, wondering where to go next. Imagine their astonishment, he recounted, when they received a call from the French embassy. Could George call on their trade attaché to discuss a matter of the gravest importance?

It was the story of what followed that I decided to tell my soon-to-be-adoptive family at this, my first French Christmas dinner.

George's first reaction to the summons from the embassy was confusion.

"The trade attaché? You don't mean the cultural at-taché?"

No, it was M. Dubois of the Trade Desk who desired to see him. And yes, it was George Johnston, the writer, they wanted.

M. Dubois had a sad story to tell. During the Nazi occupation, French *vignerons* continued to make wine. Millions of litres had accumulated, far more than Europe could ever drink. They were looking for alternative markets. Australia, perhaps?

"Australians do like a drink," George conceded, "but mainly beer. They don't go much on . . ."

He barely stopped himself using the disdainful term "plonk". Australian soldiers in France during World War I learned to ask for *"van blonk"*, and the name survived as a generic term for any alcoholic drink made out of grapes, from Gewürztraminer to Amontillado.

". . . er, wine," he finished lamely.

"Ah, that is where you come in, M'sieur Johnston," the diplomat said. "We wish to commission a series of articles about French wine for Australian newspapers and magazines. If this creates a demand, we could ship it to your country in quantity, by tanker."

George hesitated. The plan sounded crazy to him. Australians abandoning beer for *vin ordinaire*? Obviously M. Dubois had never seen an Australian

pub on a hot Saturday afternoon, with drinkers sluic-
ing down pint after pint of icy, gullet-numbing lager. He
would be doing French winemakers a favour by nipping
this scheme in the bud. On the other hand, times were
thin, and he needed the work.

"I'm no expert on French vintages," he temporised.

But Dubois was ahead of him. They would send him
to France, all expenses paid, for a tasting tour. Would he
be interested?

Savouring the moment more than twenty years later,
George lit another cigarette. "I thought back over my
life," he told me. "I'd done many contemptible things,
but obviously, somewhere, somehow, I'd performed a
good deed. And this was my reward."

The trip to France—the little he remembered of
it—was a boozer's dream. At every château throughout
Burgundy, the Loire, and the Rhône, the *propriétaire*—
sometimes a count or a duke, occasionally a prince—
waited to greet him. This, after all, was the Australian
who was going to make them rich.

In scraps of fractured movie French, with frequent
translations from Marie-Dominique, and illustrated with
gestures, noises, much waving of arms, and badly acted
impressions of French aristocrats and decrepit somme-
liers, I recounted George's adventures in the vineyards
of France that bitter, fog-bound winter.

Around the table, forks and glasses were poised half-way to lips as people struggled to follow what I said. Once I got to explaining his experience with wine, story-telling became easier. I could mime glasses being filled, tasted, filled again. And it was no problem to act out George's increasing inebriation, the out-of-focus eyes, the slurring voice.

For George, the tour became the fulfilment of every drinker's fantasy. Wine was consumed by the gallon rather than the glass, and all of it wonderful. By the time he reached the great vineyards around Bordeaux, he could barely remember who—let alone where—he was. So it was with some alarm, following another wine-logged dinner, that his host—George rather thought it had been Baron Robert de Rothschild—rose and cour-teously conducted him into the ancient *caves* cut into the clay and gravel of the Médoc.

After winding through corridors and tunnels so complex they'd defeated even the ingenuity of the Nazis, they arrived in a tiny chamber where, waiting for them, was, in George's words, "the *oldest* old fart I'd ever seen".

M. Petitjean, explained the baron, had directed wine-making in these vineyards in his father's time. Long re-tired, he'd come in tonight to see George and to show him "something interesting".

George

The old man held up a bottle. In shape, it differed from modern wine bottles in being wider and more squat, with a longer neck. Though dust obscured the faded label, George made out the number: 1812. Napoleon still ruled Europe when this was bottled.

George was about to make all the appropriate noises of appreciation at this antique when, to his consternation, the old man produced a corkscrew and began to open it. He watched in alarm as, with minute care, a spoonful of straw-coloured liquid was decanted into a glass.

George regarded it in confusion. "A *white* wine?"

The baron winced. Naturally not. This was the legendary 1812 Bordeaux. Over the decades, its solids had settled out into a black sludge, leaving only this pale plasma. And this, the last surviving bottle, as far as they could discover, had been saved for George Johnston to drink.

For the first time, George noticed he held the only glass.

"But . . . you'll taste it with me?"

The baron's shrug blended appreciation of the generosity of the offer with regret at the impossibility of acceptance. The honour of this historic degustation belonged to their guest alone.

"Well, I took a sip," George told me, "but my palate was so buggered, not only with the wine I'd drunk that week but the years of arak and jungle juice and sake and bad scotch, that it didn't taste of anything."

Petitjean and the baron were waiting. Honour was at stake.

"My skills as a drinker had deserted me," George lamented, "but I thought my skills as a writer might save the day."

"Gentlemen," he said at last, "how can I put this?"

He held the glass up to the light.

"Perhaps, like me, you have attended the farewell concert of some great old baritone at the end of a long career."

The two men frowned. What had this to do with Bordeaux?

"This wine," he went on, "reminds me of that baritone. The voice is gone—and yet, now and then, and faintly, one hears a pure and perfect note."

The baron was silent for a moment. Then he translated for M. Petitjean. Spontaneously, the old man stepped forward and kissed George on both cheeks.

I reached the end of the story feeling as if I had just hauled a wardrobe up six flights of stairs. There was silence around the table.

Looking up, I caught the eye of Jean-Paul, the elder statesman of the family, who was staring at me down the table.

Then he smiled, and lifted his glass in a toast.

"Voici un bonne raconteur," he said. *Here is a good story-teller.*

Suddenly everyone else was smiling, too, and talking at once. *Madame* bolted, beaming, for the kitchen, to serve the guinea fowl.

Under the table, Marie-Do squeezed my hand.

After dinner, as people sipped a *digestif* of cognac, wandered around the room, or gossiped by the big windows looking out into the darkened garden, Jean-Paul strolled over and sat down next to us.

"Et votre ami, l'écrivain," he inquired. *"Il est encore vivant?"*

My friend the writer still alive? No, I explained. Both George and Charmian were dead. In 1969, on the eve of the publication of the second book in George's trilogy, *Clean Straw for Nothing*, which traced the tangled sex life of a perfunctorily fictionalised Charmian, she washed down an overdose of sleeping pills with alcohol and lay down on the couch in her study to die alone. He survived her for only one more year.

In a gesture of startling intimacy for one so formal, Jean-Paul patted me on the shoulder.

"But he lives," he said in halting English. "He lives here, tonight."

By February of the following year, Marie-Dominique was pregnant. Louise Virginie Caroline—"Virginie" for my sister Virginia, "Caroline" for Marie-Dominique's sister—was born in October. The following June, we were married in the fourteenth-century church of Richebourg. And in between, on the occasion of my second December in France, in a far more potent acknowledgment of my standing in the family than any certificate of marriage or baptism, the duty of cooking Christmas dinner passed to me. I've been doing it ever since.

4

Ninety Degrees of Christmas

Church bells o'er the Darling Ranges ...
Flora gloriously rejoicing, reigning triumphant and
welcoming Santa Claus to Australia...The feathered tribes—
black swans, lady companions, kangaroos, and Aboriginals
negotiating a Christmas corrobboree.

—JOSEPH SUMMERS

A few years ago, Australian friends came to visit us in
Paris over Christmas.

"If you were at home now," I asked, "what would you
be having for lunch?"

"Well, since it's high summer out there . . ." said the
husband.

". . . and the temperature's at least ninety degrees
Fahrenheit . . ." added his wife.

". . . with bushfires everywhere . . ."

". . . we'd probably go for something cold . . ."

". . . some nice shrimp and oysters . . . maybe a lobster . . ."

". . . with a green salad . . ."

"And for dessert?"

They stared at me. *Silly question.* "A Pavlova, naturally."

There were few social occasions in Australia where it would not be appropriate to prepare this tooth-achingly sugary concoction of whipped cream and fruit salad in a boat of meringue. I had even served it myself occasionally at French dinner parties, to general enthusiasm.

And yet, whatever my friends said, a Christmas lunch of seafood and Pavlova was a relatively recent development in Australian culture.

Quite the contrary, in my childhood, an extended and indigestible English-style Christmas meal was obligatory, to be endured as a sign that the old values of Queen and Empire still thrived. This was a country where older people still spoke of England as "home", even though they had never visited it, and, when the queen's Christmas message was broadcast on the radio, solemnly stood to listen.

Driven by the same impulse to respect the British way of life, Australians ignored the fact that almost every tree on the continent was a eucalypt and raked up a scraggy conifer on which to hang our hoarded decorations. For the twelve days of Christmas, this reminder of the European winter drooped in a corner of the living room, shedding needles onto the carpet. Festoons of tinsel yellowed in the heat while strings of fairy lights glimmered feebly in sunlight so powerful it seeped through even the thickest curtains.

If we hesitated in our celebration of a feast whose roots lay in the ritual sacrifices of neolithic Scandinavia, commerce stood ready to spur us on. By October, cardboard Santas and boxes of Christmas

crackers had appeared in the newsagents. Butchers urged us to order our turkeys and hams. And also in October, at the height of the Australian spring, some seasonal impulse nudged my mother into creating her puddings.

It took days for her to assemble, weigh, and amalgamate the fats and carbohydrates, dried and preserved fruits and rinds, the liqueurs and spices that went into these potent examples of traditional northern European Christmas cuisine. As a kid, I was given the job of mixing the batter. I can still feel the gluey yellow/brown paste between my fingers, gritty with sugar but at the same time slick with butter. Ironically, years later, I tasted an almost identical mixture of sugar, fat, and spice in that potent Swedish Christmas drink, glögg. Between the dark northern woods and the gums of the Australian bush, the degrees of separation were not as numerous as I'd thought.

Once the mix was completed, she exhumed from a bottom drawer half a dozen "pudding cloths". Squares cut from the remains of ancient linen teatowels, they were stiff as parchment, "seasoned" with repeated use. Each one, freshly dusted with flour, was allocated a dollop of the paste, into which, before it was gathered into a bundle with a loop of string, a sixpenny piece, boiled free of germs, was dropped.

Attached by their strings, these bundles were suspended in boiling water from a broom handle placed across the largest pot we owned. After simmering them for hours, she lifted them out and hung them to "season" from the shower rail in the bathroom. They remained there until Christmas day, when the cloth was peeled off, and the pudding carried ritually to the table, doused in burning brandy, the blue flames dancing feebly in the summer light.

Their firm, slightly gelatinous consistency, more like heavy aspic than cake, and achieved, I later learned, by substituting white bread crumbs for some of the flour, made her puddings delicious both hot and cold. The two or three she made never lasted through the holidays. Creeping downstairs in the dawn of Boxing Day, hoping for a few quiet, cool hours before the heat descended and the flies rose, one would surprise a family member standing in robe and slippers before the open refrigerator, guiltily forking up the last crumbs of a plateful.

For years before moving to France, I battled, without conspicuous success, against our Australian family Christmas. But whatever inroads I made—sneaking in a capon or goose, for instance, instead of the dry, tasteless turkey—the pudding stood foursquare and impregnable, a fortification behind which my parents could retreat, confident no culinary artillery would make a dent.

During the 1970s, living in England, I succumbed at

last, and decided to make my own. Extracting the recipe from my mother, I corralled the ingredients—far easier in London, I thought smugly, than in rural Australia— and boiled up a single example, which I hung behind the shower curtain in my minuscule bathroom. Returning from a trip a few days before Christmas, I checked—to find it invaded by blue-grey mould. Dumping the musty failure in the garbage, I bought a ready-made one at Harrod's.

A decade later, returning to Australia with Marie-Dominique, I once again shared Christmas dinner with my parents. Wandering into the bathroom, I studied the puddings dangling from the shower rail—all plump, fragrant, and free of mould. Had my mother omitted some crucial ingredient from the recipe she sent me? Or did the desiccated Australian air act as a fungicide? Maybe if I'd exposed mine to the BBC broadcast of a cricket Test match, or read aloud a few verses of *The Man from Snowy River*?

I never discovered her secret, since at that moment my father called from the living room, "That wine of yours is still in the garage."

"What wine?"

"Don't you remember? Before you left, you gave me some wine to look after."

I thought back ten years. In those days, I'd been a

partner in a syndicate that bought up the cellars of bankrupt restaurants and hotels. We split the profits, with the bonus of a few choice bottles kept back for our own use. Such a deal had been closed just before I left for England, and I vaguely remembered asking my father to mind my allocation—a little like asking a rabbit to guard the lettuce patch.

"I thought you'd have drunk it," I said.

"No fear! It's still out there."

Rummaging in the depths of the garage, we unearthed the now-rotted cardboard carton, with its bottles fortunately intact. I carried them into the light.

In 1969, these wines had been respectable. Ten years had turned them into classics. And, paradoxically, the dark and damp under abandoned tents and unused sporting equipment at the back of a garage provided the ideal environment for their preservation.

There was a half-bottle of French Sauternes—not Château d'Yquem but, from the honeyed richness of the colour, a delight all the same, particularly accompanying a slice of foie gras. Then a respectable château-bottled Pomerol of 1968, an Echezaux Burgundy of 1966, and an Alsatian Spatlese Riesling that, while past its best, was probably still drinkable.

And the last.

Hardly believing my luck, I carried it with reverence

into the kitchen and wiped the dust and cobwebs from its plain beige label.

"That's not a Grange?" said my brother-in-law incredulously.

It was indeed a 1962 bottle of Penfolds Grange Hermitage, the most valued of all Australian reds, the shiraz that, in the opinion of Robert Parker, a fanatic for French vintages, "replaced Bordeaux's Pétrus as the world's most exotic and concentrated wine".

Bottles of Grange changed hands for hundreds, even thousands of dollars. Their owners treated them like pedigreed animals. Penfolds maintained a clinic that would advise on, sample, and, if necessary, recork your bottle.

A phone call to an oenophile friend established that the 1962 Grange was worth about AU$1,000 at auction—and in a restaurant, double or triple that.

"If you want to sell it," he said, trying to keep the hunger out of his voice, "I wouldn't mind giving myself a little late Christmas present."

We sat around the kitchen and contemplated this windfall.

Of course I should sell it—not only because of its monetary value but because such a wine simply didn't belong in the context of an Australian Christmas lunch. It cried out for linen and silver and fumed oak, not paper napkins and Formica; for rare beef and *gratin dauphinois*, not battery turkey and roasted spuds; not the squawk of currawongs and a whiff of a bushfire wafting through the window, but the strains of Benjamin Britten on the evening air, and the smoke from a good cigar.

But if living in Europe had taught me anything, it was the pointlessness of straining to attain someone else's standards. It was not only our right but our duty to take pleasure gratefully when and wherever it was offered.

"It should breathe a bit," I said, reaching for the corkscrew.

The wine was sublime, an explosion on the palate, with, as the Japanese say, a tail that went right down the throat. Each sip recalled something said by the seventeenth-century poet George Herbert but adopted as a motto by Gerald and Sara Murphy, friends of Scott and Zelda Fitzgerald and the inspiration for Dick and Nicole Diver in *Tender Is the Night*: "Living well is the best revenge."

And here's a funny thing: it went particularly well with Christmas pudding.

5

The Food of Love

There are three possible parts to a date, of which at least
two must be offered: entertainment, food, and affection. It
is customary to begin a series of dates with a great deal of
entertainment, a moderate amount of food, and the merest
suggestion of affection. As the amount of affection increases,
the entertainment can be reduced proportionately. When
the affection is the entertainment, we no longer call it dating.
Under no circumstances can the food be omitted.

—JUDITH MARTIN

Cooking for myself began as a means of survival.

Living alone as a young man in Sydney during the
early 1960s was an incentive to learn at least the rudi-
ments of cuisine, and I could soon assemble a serviceable
three-course dinner. Though none of my "signature

dishes" would excite comment today, all were remote from standard Aussie fare, which embodied one simple rule: on finding any raw meat or vegetable, plunge it immediately into boiling salt water and hold down the lid until it ceased to struggle.

My roast shoulder of lamb was pink in the centre, spiked with garlic and scattered with fresh rosemary. I served it with steamed asparagus and hollandaise sauce, or an Italian potato salad with dried herbs and sweet onions, dressed not with the standard store-bought mayonnaise but with olive oil—in those days an ingredient so exotic that no markets stocked it. The most convenient source was pharmacies, where it was sold as a treatment for dry scalp and removing ear wax.

This salad was the first recipe I ever learned. I was ten and living in an inner-city suburb just being colonised by the first Italians to make the long journey from war-ruined Europe to a new life on the other side of the world. One of the single-storey Victorian terraced houses opposite housed such a family, dominated by a young but determined mother who spent most of her time in the kitchen. None of them spoke English, but I struck up a friendship with one of the boys, on the strength of which I was invited to eat lunch.

I've forgotten nothing about that meal. Who could? If this was what Venusians ate, it could not have been

more alien and exotic. There was spaghetti—a dish I knew only as it came in a Heinz can, cooked to mush and doused in tomato sauce. This was fresh from the pot, and chewy, baptised with oil and garlic, and a pungent grated cheese that smelled like sick but tasted sublime. Their homemade bread wasn't spongy and white but crusty, dusted with flour, and delicious if you dipped it, as my hostess demonstrated, in olive oil and salt.

As for that extraordinary dish of lukewarm boiled potatoes, raw onion, herbs, oil, and vinegar, I made a pig of myself, and was back the next day in hopes of more. Instead, my friend's mother—whose name I never learned but always referred to as "Mary Over the Road"—gave me the greatest gift one can confer on any lover of food: she showed me how to make it.

Cooking for women began as an economy—who could afford a good restaurant for every date?—but the reaction of the first few girlfriends for whom I prepared a meal alerted me to the possibilities.

"You really made this yourself?" they'd say, leaning in the kitchen doorway, glass of wine in hand, surreptitiously glancing around for frozen-food packs or Tupperware containers that might suggest I'd smuggled in dishes prepared by my mother.

"Sure."

At this point, I'd splash some wine into the hot pan, dissolving the juices in preparation for a sauce. If you tilted the pan with one hand and tipped the bottle with the other, using your thumb as a stopper, it not only looked casually expert but resulted in a hiss of steam, a puff of blue flame—and, with luck, a squeal from your date.

Theatrics kept them amused, and it helped that the food tasted good, but neither counted for as much as the fact that I'd cooked for them. Educated to serve men—this was long before "Ms." came into use or a single bra was burned—they found it disturbingly satisfying to be served by one. For every woman mesmerised by a sports-man flexing his bicep and saying "Feel that", a dozen yearned to be cosseted, entertained—and fed.

Among my friends, however, the use of cooking for seduction was heretical. They could only imagine food having an erotic effect if it contained some proven aph-rodisiac, like the legendary cantharides or Spanish fly. Other ingredients reputed to improve potency were oysters, asparagus, liquorice, and celery. According to the banned *Kama Sutra*, ill-translated copies of which, greasy and stained, circulated clandestinely, the problem at its most extreme responded to goats' testicles boiled in milk—now *there's* a Breakfast of Champions—while men in more dire need could turn to desiccated tiger pe-nis and powdered rhinoceros horn.

The man who lifted the curse of campiness from cooking was Graham Kerr, the first celebrity chef to ap-pear on Australian TV. He popularised that wine-in-the-pan manoeuvre, and regular Aussies were reassured about the sexual orientation of cooks by his claim that any dish, from chicken soup to cornflakes, could be im-proved by "a short slurp of sherry." Since an ability to hold your liquor was sure proof of masculinity, anyone who drank like Kerr had to be an authentic male. (Too authentic, perhaps, since in later years he confessed to longtime alcoholism.)

Though Kerr taught me how to look like a cook, my first real culinary teacher was British chef Philip Harben. The Penguin paperback of his cookbook became my key to the world of cuisine. Small, bearded, intense, Harben wrote about cooking with the passion of a true believer. In addition to being an historian of food—one of his specialities was to prepare a banquet in the style of the Tudors—he was a physicist of cuisine, a kitchen chemist.

Rather than dictating recipes, he explained how food *worked*. Why does flour thicken a sauce? What makes oil and egg yolk blend into mayonnaise? Why does heat make meat brown? His answers raised such related questions—crucial to the true cook—as "What if you don't *have* any flour?" and "What if your mayonnaise separates?" Thanks to him, I can open the kitchen cupboard in a strange apartment, take a packet or two, and, with the help of an egg and a lemon, assemble a dinner.

He taught that fresh sweetcorn *improved* if boiled for only a minute or two rather than the half-hour usually advised, and is even better if you sugar the water rather than salt it. Frozen peas, which are chilled before their sugars can turn to starch, are more tender than any but the freshest of store-bought peas—and, moreover, benefit from being cooked without water, in a closed pan, in their own steam, with nothing but some butter and a sprig of fresh mint.

As for meat, long cooking doesn't tenderise flesh but shrinks it, forcing out the juices, creating the "tough-as-old-boots beefsteak" familiar to me since childhood. Good beef is more tender the *less* it is cooked and can even, suggested Harben, be eaten *raw*—an unimaginable heresy in Australia, where everyone I knew shrank from any sign of pinkness in meat and greeted the presence of natural juices with a shudder and the cry "Ugh! Blood!"

Not surprisingly, food first brought me together with my future wife, Marie-Dominique.

It was 1974. I was a visiting professor at Hollins College in Roanoke, Virginia, and she a recent graduate of the Sorbonne, spending a "gap" year in the United States while she decided what to do with her life.

I was smitten the first instant I met her, but any designs I might have had were frustrated by a looming boyfriend from Chicago for whom she showed an incomprehensible preference. Once he'd gone, I made it my business to get to know her. Finding that we shared an enthusiasm for certain French films, I invited her around for dinner and a movie.

She ate my lamb without comment, and liked my asparagus well enough, but inquired, "You always serve it with hollandaise?"

"Sometimes with melted butter."

"Have you tried it with a vinaigrette?"

"You mean cold, like a salad?"

"No, *tiède* . . . lukewarm. As an entrée."

Occasionally, women disliked what I cooked, but having one discuss the ingredients and offer suggestions was a new experience—and not, I was surprised to find, disagreeable. Clearly there was something about Frenchwomen—or this particular Frenchwoman?—that couldn't be discovered by the simple expedient of cooking them a meal.

The next time she came to lunch, I served asparagus again, this time with a vinaigrette.

"It is quite good." Her tone suggested it wasn't *that* good. "Do you ever put egg in your vinaigrette?"

"Hard-boiled?"

"Let me show you."

Taking the bowl of French dressing, she went into the kitchen, cracked an egg, separated the yolk, and dropped it into the oil and vinegar.

"You have some mustard?"

I silently handed her the Grey Poupon. She spooned some into the mixture and whisked it for a few seconds.

My watery-looking mixture of oil, vinegar, and salt was transformed into a creamy golden emulsion.

"Taste."

She dipped her forefinger into it and held it up. I licked it.

The dressing tasted delicious.

So did her finger.

We didn't marry for another fifteen years, but our courtship began with that finger and that vinaigrette.

6

The Servant Problem

Pas devant les domestiques! (Not in front of the servants)
—TRADITIONAL FRENCH EXHORTATION

On a chill morning the week before Christmas 2007, Marie-Do and I drove out of rue de l'Odéon and headed south for the *périphérique*, the ring road that circles Paris. Five hours later, we arrived at our summer house in Fouras on the Atlantic coast.

Business took us there, and, for me, at the very worst time, since I should have been shopping for the ingredients to create my Christmas banquet.

A gust from the ocean cuffed the car as we circled the small square and parked under the spreading lime trees flanking the front gate. The leaves that in summer dappled coins of sunlight on the pavement were now fallen and dead. Others had gathered in sodden drifts on the terrace under our grape arbour, leaving the vines, stripped of greenery, looking as shrunken, brown, and contorted as the arms of old men.

Marie-Dominique's grandparents left her the house, their retirement home, in their will. Built at the end of the nineteenth century, it stood in a small walled garden dominated by an ancient pear tree. In one corner, a pavilion, little more than a chill stone shed with a tiled roof, recalled the days before refrigerators, when game could hang for days until properly rotted, and apples mellowed in the cool dark.

The house preserved for her all the memories and certainties of childhood, which had ended abruptly when she was nine, and her father, deported to Germany during the war as slave labour, died of the tuberculosis he contracted there. As a young journalist, she'd lived in a tiny one-room studio in Paris, spending every franc she could afford on replacing Fouras's crumbling roof and searching out antique furniture and linen appropriate to the year it was built.

For each summer of my eighteen years in France, we'd come here in mid-July, only departing, and then reluctantly, in the last days of August. My memories of the house were a compendium of sunlight and heat, of hours spent reading in a deckchair under the big *poirier*,

a glass of Campari and orange juice at hand, the only interruption a thud as one of the small, hard, inedible pears hit the ground.

But now, instead of the sounds of summer—chattering kids passing on their way to the beach, vans with loudspeakers bawling a summons to the night's *Guignol* or *marche de nuit*—there was only a drone of wind. It carried the tang of salt, and a sense of limitless grey water rolling under a sullen sky.

A few years before, the same wind swept across France in a gale that ripped off roofs and chimneys, uprooted trees, and overturned cars. Sylvie, our Fouras housekeeper for years, rousted her handyman boyfriend out of bed at two a.m. to repair the roof and forestall further damage. Unfortunately for us, she subsequently decided to retire. Since then, we'd grappled with a series of *gardiennes*, none of whom registered above "adequate" on the competence scale. Looking for Mary Poppins, we invariably got Mrs. Doubtfire.

Sylvie, though no longer a candidate, regarded it as her duty to vet her replacements. Of the latest, so new we knew her only as Madame Becker, she said, "She seems all right. If she'd get out of those stilettos."

Imagining someone vacuuming in stiletto heels gave a new and piquant perspective to the concept of house-work, but that was before I met Madame Becker. Her high heels proved to be the most exciting thing about her, with some heavily lacquered red hair running a close second. In her forties, and apparently widowed, she was an-other of those people who, displaced from the city by bad luck or worse judgment, end up in a seaside town. With no other work available, they accept jobs far below their social or intellectual level. We were used to child-minders with half a college degree who'd been left stranded here by a runaway boyfriend and a baby, or women who re-tired with a husband, only to have him decamp or drop dead, leaving them with a big house and only a small an-nuity on which to maintain it and themselves.

From Paris, we'd rung Madame Becker, asking her to prepare the house for our stay, taking down the shut-ters, switching on the heat, and stocking the refrigerator with basics. Our arrival, a few hours earlier than planned, caught her on the wrong foot. The shutters were still up, the fridge empty, the floors unswept. The only signs she'd been near the place in weeks were an ashtray filled with Marlboro butts and an empty three-litre box of *vin rosé*.

As I carried the bags from the car, Marie-Do prowled the rooms, slamming doors, muttering, her voice rising periodically to a cry of frustration at some new example of neglect.

About hired help, she and I had exactly opposite ideas. The previous summer, I had barely stopped her from firing M. Courtepaille, an eccentric young local who'd rebuilt our kitchen and bathroom. He did the work well enough, but, as he told it later, a leak had soaked some cartons of wine placed in the *cave*.

"The cardboard was wet," he explained, "and when I lifted it up, it broke."

"The whole carton?" I said. "A dozen bottles?" I'd suffered similar accidents myself, but a few bottles always survived.

"Afraid so," he said, staring me in the eye. "Every last one."

"That was a Margaux '96," I said. "You know what it's worth?"

"I couldn't be more sorry." *Or more of a liar.*

Marie-Do would have fired him on the spot, but I intervened. *After all,* I told myself, *would I, in similar circumstances, have resisted the temptation?* But this was just an evasion. Egalitarian Australia has a national problem with employees and servants, which I had inherited. Is there any other country where cab passengers automatically take the seat next to the driver? To ride in the back would indicate an unearned sense of superiority. When, in Preston Sturges's *The Palm Beach Story*, the millionaire played by Rudy Vallee refuses to ride first-class on the train—"Staterooms are un-American!"—I know exactly how he feels.

When I arrived in Paris, it shook me somewhat that Marie-Dominique had a pretty black maid from Réunion named May, who slipped in early in the morning to brew coffee and squeeze orange juice, then make the bed and do the washing and the shopping. However, just as I decided that my discomfort reflected outmoded colonial attitudes, and this was, after all, a simple commercial relationship, hints appeared that made me change my mind. Despite their apparent insouciance, the French are deeply ambivalent about servants. Every few years, some filmmaker or novelist rakes up the story of Lea and Christine Papin, the maids who butchered their employer and her daughter in Le Mans in 1933. Jean Genet's play *The Maids* shows the sisters repeatedly acting out the crime before they commit it. Each rehearsal increases their hatred, until, when they do strike, it is with fury. (In real life, the Papins gouged out the eyes of their victims and mutilated the corpses, after which they neatly cleaned up and went to bed, making no attempt to escape.) The cold-bloodedness of the crime bore a dismaying moral: *Our servants hate us. They'd kill us if they dared.*

Through my years in France, I'd accepted the necessity of having a housekeeper, but some of my old concerns returned as we waited for Madame Becker, whom Marie-Do had summoned with an icy phone call. Hearing her car arrive and her heels click on the pavement outside our front gate, I found an excuse to go upstairs. This was something only a Frenchwoman could handle.

Most of what followed I half-heard as it filtered up through the floorboards. The conversation swelled and diminished as they moved from room to room, in each of which Marie-Dominique paused to enumerate the deficiencies of care. At every moment, I expected to hear the declaration that *Madame* was *virée*—fired—but each time the recital of complaint and excuse flowed on.

After half an hour, her heels receded and our gate creaked shut. Looking out the window, I saw her car accelerating away, the only sign of her departure the empty wine box, now lying defiantly in the gutter in front of the house.

I went back downstairs. "Are we looking for a new housekeeper?"

"We'll see. She says she's going to find some firewood. And produce some food."

"On the Friday before Christmas? From where?"

"That's her problem."

For half an hour, we pottered about, restoring habitability to the house. We were just done when a car pulled up and, a moment later, a clatter brought us to the window. Madame Becker, still dressed in high heels, a fur-collared overcoat, and kid gloves, as if on her way to church, was dumping a pile of logs by the door. By the time we reached the kitchen, she was on her way out the gate.

"Bon appétit," she said over her shoulder.

On the table she had left a baguette, a bottle of milk, a slab of butter, lettuce, and a bowl of pale pink salt-water crayfish. I touched one. It was still warm from the water in which it had been boiled.

"Langoustines," I said reverently.

The langoustine, a miniature lobster, is trawled from the waters just off Fouras. It's larger than a shrimp and longer than the American or Australian crayfish, with two hard, elongated claws and a stubby body. Every summer, langoustines were piled in great squirming heaps in the local fish market. We bought them by the kilo, plunged them into salted water flavoured with a bay leaf and an onion, then gorged ourselves on dozens each, with homemade mayonnaise and a baguette.

"Do you suppose this was *her* dinner?" I knew it was absurd the moment I said it. Madame wasn't the self-sacrificing type.

"No," said Marie-Do thoughtfully. "But maybe her lover's?"

That made more sense. For a woman, Frenchmen would sacrifice much more than their dinner. I spared a thought for this individual, no doubt morosely settling down to a cold supper of bread and cheese. Hopefully, however, his reward for this self-sacrifice would be worth it.

As with most French food, there is an approved technique for eating the langoustine. One first tears it in two, separating the head and claws from the stumpy body. The meat of the body, tender and sweet, is extracted by squeezing the shell until it cracks, then edging out the nugget of white flesh.

This leaves the claws, from which one can, if one has the energy, winkle a little more meat with a probe. But if you're *really* serious about langoustines, like my mother-in-law, you take the head, put the severed end to your lips, and slurp out the juice.

I got used to having servants. But I never got used to that.

• • •

Over supper, my thoughts turned again to Christmas dinner.

There are always two possible strategies in preparing a meal for the French.

One was novelty. I could present the family with something so exotic that sheer strangeness would keep them interested. I'd done this a few times when I first cooked in France. At various times, dinner guests had been treated to Indian curries, Thai shrimp salad, and Mexican chicken with bitter chocolate mole sauce. We had once—not an experience to be repeated—even taken them to an Australian restaurant that served kangaroo.

Most had been polite. A few had been appreciative. But one sensed a general feeling that I was trying too hard to impress.

Which brought me to the second and far more demanding option—tradition.

Anyone who takes on classic French cooking faces a formidable challenge. Whatever its reputation for rich sauces and flashy presentation, French cuisine, I'd come to understand through painful experience, is essentially simple. It relies on precisely isolating and emphasising the essential flavour of an ingredient, then juxtaposing two or more such tastes in a pleasing or surprising harmony. Who else but the French would think of cutting the fattiness of foie gras with a sweet, chill glass of Sauternes? Or serving scrambled eggs with the roe of the sea urchin?

Seasonality and regionality also count for a lot. Better to eat local *girolles* or *coeur de pigeon* cherries during their brief seasons than imported Romanian or Spanish equivalents. And no satisfaction is greater than serving game shot on your own *terroir*, fish caught in your own river, or fruit picked in a local orchard.

The pleasure the French take in this was underlined for me the previous summer, a week of which we spent in Cambridge. In soaking rain, we drove to Calais to take the Dover ferry. Along every kilometre of the narrow roads of Picardy, men and women in raincoats browsed the grass verges with plastic bags, gathering snails—a familiar sight on any warm wet day in France. But, on the British side of the Channel, an identical landscape in identical weather, the verges, no doubt just as crowded with snails, were deserted.

The supper Marie-Do and I were enjoying showed that, even in winter, the French *terroir* continued to produce the best ingredient. These langoustines, this bread, butter, and wine all came from within a few kilometres of where we ate them. Why shouldn't my Christmas dinner comprise dishes that represented *all* of France, not simply the island of specialised taste that was Paris?

It was a challenge. But that was the fun of it. As I winkled a nugget of orange roe from the head of a hen langoustine and smeared it on some baguette with a glob of mayonnaise, I began yet again to replan the menu.

7

The Ghosts of Christmases Past

Christmas? Bah! Humbug!

—CHARLES DICKENS

Until I moved to France, Christmas was not a season I viewed with affection or anticipated with pleasure.

A solitary child, I lived in books and movies—and the Christmas in books and movies, invariably European or American, was not the Christmas I saw through the window. Where was bleak midwinter? The stockings all hung by the chimney with care? The Ghost of Christmas Past and Tiny Tim and "God bless us every one"? Watching Judy Garland sing "Have Yourself a Merry Little Christmas" in the movie *Meet Me in St. Louis* or reading of Christmas among the small animals of the English countryside in *The Wind in the Willows* could move me to tears, but for the blazing sun of the Australian December, I shed not a drop.

Some of my warmest Christmas memories were of those times when I'd avoided it entirely, when, for instance, living in Los Angeles in the 1980s, I briefly became an international courier.

Well, I can call it that, but essentially I was a delivery boy, albeit an exalted one. Before FedEx and other express shippers cornered the market, certain companies that needed to move documents across the world in bulk and in a hurry—large legal firms, in particular—used couriers. In return for the use of our baggage allowance, we received an air ticket to wherever the papers needed to go. This was the pinnacle of unskilled labour. Provided we had a passport and were willing to cross the world with just a toothbrush and a change of underwear, we got the job. The trick, as with much else in the world, was in knowing such jobs existed and, more important, being friendly with the people who handed them out.

In December 1988 I was alone in Los Angeles and contemplating another joyless Christmas when my friend at the courier agency rang. She had documents for Australia, but nobody wanted to take them over the holidays. Could I accompany a shipment to Sydney on Christmas Eve?

VOYAGE EN VIEILLE FRANCE

There was an exhilarating sense of freedom in boarding a Boeing at LAX with only an overnight bag as hand luggage. Whirling in my wake as it took off were all thoughts of gifts, cards, trees, carols, eggnog, turkey, Santa, and screenings of *It's a Wonderful Life*.

After an entire day in the air, I landed at Sydney's Kingsford Smith Terminal. Breezing through the "Returning Australian Citizens" lane of passport control, I left my fellow passengers to loiter around the baggage carousels, strolled through customs, and delivered my luggage tickets to a frazzled-looking legal secretary. Within half an hour of touchdown, at the start of what promised to be a scorching summer morning, I was in an air-conditioned cab heading for the house of a friend. Conveniently, she wasn't even out of bed when I arrived, and we didn't leave it for most of the weekend. I remember that particular Christmas as brimming with comfort and joy, and not a reindeer in sight.

But such happy occasions were rare. To be unattached and far from home during the holiday season is generally to be a leper. Despair trails you like a miasma, infecting everyone.

It's almost worse when friends take pity. They squeeze in an extra chair at the Christmas lunch, and, rather than see you excluded from the oohs, aahs, and cries of "Oh, you shouldn't have!" around the Christmas tree, rake out a few of last year's unused or unwanted gifts. ("Let's give him this. You've never worn it.")

Only one writer, to my knowledge, positively relished the idea of a lone Christmas far from home. Samuel Beckett, in London to rehearse the 1979 premiere of *Happy Days* at the Royal Court Theatre, announced to the director's assistant Anton Gill that he wouldn't bother returning to Paris for Christmas but would stay in London. Anton invited him to spend Christmas with his family, but Beckett politely declined.

When rehearsals recommenced the following week, Anton asked, "How did you spend Christmas, Sam?"

Beckett regarded him with his customary weary melancholy.

"Oh, I just walked around London," he said, "revisiting the old places."

"Well, I hope you enjoyed a good Christmas dinner," Anton said.

It was like asking the Archbishop of Canterbury whether he'd taken the opportunity of a trip to California to visit Disneyland.

"A little boiled fish," said a pained Beckett, "in my room."

"If that hadn't been so *exactly* what one would expect him to say," Anton recalls, "I would almost have believed it." But he could never entirely dispel an image of the austere Beckett, napkin tucked into his collar, in some big London restaurant, like Simpson's in the Strand, stuffing himself with roast turkey and Christmas pudding, washed down with a quart of Guinness.

For many years, my American wife, Joyce, and I lived in north London. Having calculatedly severed ourselves from our roots, we imagined our neighbours, also mostly childless couples in middle management or the arts, had done the same. Yet the night before Christmas, our streets emptied of parked cars, even the most ancient bangers, as these hardened city-dwellers, like salmon swimming upstream, headed back to their family homes for the holidays.

One Christmas, hoping to strike a blow for a less family-oriented festival, we threw a lunch for a dozen unattached friends who were, like ourselves, alone in London.

The occasion could have been more cheerless, I suppose—if, for instance, we served cold mutton, mutton soup, and bananas (the menu that drove Lizzie Borden to take a hatchet to her parents), or staged a reading from Ibsen, or invited a Jehovah's Witness to lead us in prayer. One by one, our guests, made even more miserable by booze and the Christmas television programming, subsided into armchairs, staring in silence at the walls as night drew on and scraps of old newspaper blew along the empty streets.

We did even worse on another American Christmas, this time spent in Louisville, Kentucky, where my ex-wife's mother was visiting her mother. (Divorce ran through Joyce's family like one of those genetic conditions that passes down the female line. Her grandmother, mother, and sister were all divorced, so, when she and I separated, it seemed no more than a case of succumbing to the family disease.) The plethora of discarded wives and new husbands scattered around Louisville made the city a diplomatic minefield. Socialising with one faction automatically attracted the hatred of all the others. *"I can't believe you stayed with them, after what he did to me!"*

On that particular Christmas, neither of us could face the barrage of recrimination. We decided, after calling on Joyce's mother and grandmother, to stay quietly in a hotel over Christmas and slip out of town on Boxing Day.

But on Christmas morning, a knock on the door roused me. I opened it, to be faced by a skinny African-American man in a Santa suit. Behind him stood a TV camera crew, lights blazing.

"Happy Christmas," said the sable Santa and, dipping into his sack, handed me a banana.

"Um, Merry Christmas," I said, and closed the door. Pausing a beat, I reopened it and asked, "Someone like to tell me what this is about?"

"We're from local TV news," the cameraman said. "We're doing a piece on people alone in town over the holidays."

"OK," I said. "Want to try take two?"

I closed the door, opened it to a second knock, affected surprise, accepted the banana, and answered a couple of questions about hospitable Louisville, a city I loved.

"What was that?" Joyce asked sleepily when we were done.

"Local TV."

She was suddenly alert. "You didn't *talk* to them?"

"Sure. Why not?"

"Because it'll be all over tonight's news! Now *everyone* will know we were here."

She was right, of course. This time, the complaints were exceptionally bitter. "It's bad enough you didn't call," hissed an aunt, "but to go to a *hotel* . . ."

All the time I lived in the United States, I never escaped the conviction that Americans don't celebrate Christmas at all. It's at Thanksgiving that families come together, massive meals are eaten, hatchets buried (or disinterred), affections restored, wounds healed. Christmas comes as a gaudy afterthought, an encouragement to overdo those reconciliations, to put love on a paying basis, to offer objects in place of emotions. Too often, the good done in November doesn't survive into the New Year. Maybe Europe is fortunate in having less to be thankful for.

8

Oysters

You needn't tell me that a man who doesn't love oysters
and asparagus and good wines has got a soul, or a stomach
either. He's simply got the instinct for being unhappy
highly developed.

—SAKI (H. H. MUNRO)

Fouras sits on a crooked spit of land jutting into the Atlantic. Erosion by the ocean on one side and the river Charente on the other has worn the promontory knife-blade thin, and so in danger of separation from the mainland it's earned the title *La Presqu'île*—the Almost Island.

On its river side, the town faces the watery front yard of the Charente estuary, scattered with low-lying offshore islands—Île d'Aix, Île de Ré, Île d'Oléron, Île Madame. Stone forts dating from the eighteenth century armour the shores that look out to the Atlantic, an architecture reflected in the villas that line the seafronts and nearby coastlines. Retired navy men, unable to imagine a life that didn't always turn its eyes oceanward, had crowned them with as many rooftop lookouts and widow's walks as the houses of Nantucket.

And also like New England, this is seafood country. Along the shores of the estuary, stilted fish houses, called *carrelets*, dangle wide square nets above the shallows. When the tide surges in over the mudflats, they're lowered to trap the shrimp that scramble in to feed. Children love being taken to Île d'Aix on the little ferry, where one can do the same but on a smaller scale. Wading ankle-deep into the milky water with hand nets, they sieve up shrimp so small and soft-shelled they can be boiled and eaten whole.

Above all, this is France's capital of oysters. They thrive in the cold tidal brine. At maturity, the growers transfer them to shallow ponds of fresh water where they lie for months, purging salt and ingesting a local microbe that turns their flesh a faint, translucent green—the signature of the most fancied of all French oysters, the *Charentais claire*.

"What about oysters to start Christmas dinner?" I suggested that winter, the morning after our langoustine supper.

Oysters

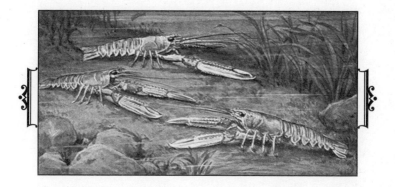

"Oysters?" Marie-Do said. "Not foie gras?"

"We have that every year." I played my trump card. "And oysters *are* traditional."

You never go far wrong in France appealing to history and the *patrimoine*. And traditionally, every Christmas dinner did begin with oysters—usually accompanied, oddly, by a side dish of small fried pork sausages. I always found this inexplicable, since the greasy, salty sausages had nothing in common with shellfish. With just as little logic, French restaurants serve oysters with a dish of red-wine vinegar and chopped shallots, guaranteed to destroy the taste as surely as the horseradish-and-ketchup "cocktail sauce" of American seafood restaurants.

"I don't think the fish market is open," Marie-Do said.

It wasn't. I'd walked past that morning. In the summer, the Napoleonic stone barn of a building overflowed with vendors selling fresh oysters and mussels, clams, sea urchins, sea snails, and hillocks of shrimp and langoustine—either cooked or alive and squirming, next to sluggish lobsters and crabs. On lazy days, we'd choose a plateful of shellfish at one of the stands and have it served under the verandah outside, with a bottle of the tart local *aligote* carried over from the Café des Marées opposite.

If one wanted fish for dinner, we could choose from a score of varieties, any one of which a *poissonnier* would fillet to order. Since most of his clients were city people who didn't cook, he'd throw in a quick lesson on how to prepare it—whether needed or not.

I was resigned to these conversations—about the *colin*, for instance, a local favourite.

"Ah, a very pretty fish," he would say, stroking the grey leathery skin of this actually quite repulsive creature. "Now, you know, the correct way to cook the *colin* . . ."

"With the tail in the mouth," I said.

". . . is with its tail in its mouth," he continued, "like this."

He started to bend its long cylindrical body into a hoop.

"Poached," I said. "In *court-bouillon*."

"Then you make a *court-bouillon*," he went on, as if

I hadn't spoken, "with white wine, water, salt, and some fresh herbs. I like *cerfeuil* myself . . ."

"Cerfeuil!" said his wife, pausing in wrapping a *darne* of salmon. "Why would *Monsieur* use *cerfeuil*? A leaf of *laurier*, a *brin* of *persil plat* . . ."

"I like *basilic* myself," interjected the woman buying the salmon.

All three of us turned to stare at her, then, eyebrows raised, at each other. Basil? In *court-bouillon*? Bizarre.

He finished wrapping the *colin* and passed it to me.

"It's very good lukewarm," he confided, "with boiled potatoes and mayonnaise"—just the way I intended to serve it. Leaning closer, and with a glance to make sure his wife couldn't hear, he said, "Really, *cerfeuil* is the thing. Believe me. Try it. Tell me if I'm not right."

Seafood lovers are legion, and passionate. The British actor Paul Freeman told me about the time he arrived in nearby La Rochelle on the morning of New Year's Day 1981, urgently summoned by Steven Spielberg to play Belloq, the cunning French archaeologist in *Raiders of the Lost Ark*. He was met by the production manager, who explained that Steve was on location in the old German submarine pens at La Pallice and couldn't see him immediately.

Freeman, noticing that a harbourside restaurant was

offering a fourteen-course seafood lunch, took a table and waited for the dishes to arrive.

"We commenced," he recalled, "with a superlative *amuse-bouche* of *pâté de saumon* on toast points . . ."

Oléron oysters followed, then langoustines with mayonnaise. He was sucking the juice out of their heads when the assistant director arrived: Spielberg had returned to his hotel and was available to see him.

"Before the *soupe au poisson?*" said Freeman. "Unthinkable."

An hour later, the assistant returned, now somewhat agitated, just as course number nine, a fragrant and deliquescent Époisses, was placed before Freeman, with a glass of muscadet.

"Steve says . . ."

"Sit down," said Freeman. "Try this cheese."

The assistant knew when he was licked. Freeman was still there, lingering over a Calvados, as the sun set behind the towers flanking the harbour entrance.

About the same time, but on the other side of the world, Italian critic and novelist Umberto Eco made it a condition of attending a conference in Australia that they give him a week's holiday on the Great Barrier Reef. His hosts complied by booking him into the luxury Heron Island resort.

Descending in his shorts late in the morning, the

tubby Eco, no respecter of mealtimes, asked if there was any chance of some oysters. The concierge directed his attention to the buffet, being piled with seafood in expectation of lunch.

"But if you want some right away . . ."

He returned, not with a plate, as Eco expected, but a small hammer.

"Just walk along there a bit, mate," he said, pointing to the nearby shore. "The rocks are thick with 'em."

Eco spent a happy hour harvesting and enjoying on the spot the freshest oysters he would ever eat.

Both Freeman and Eco shared the conviction of many of us, that work is all very well, but that something in the seasonality of seafood, its essentiality of freshness, demands our instant attention. The translucency of an oyster's flesh, the gleam of a fish's eye, and the sheen of its skin are imperatives that transcend the banality of existence, imposing a duty of relish which we, as creatures of the sea ourselves, who still weep and sweat salt, ignore at our peril. "Sometimes I dream of the seafood of Marseilles," says the Water Rat in Kenneth Grahame's *The Wind in the Willows*, "and wake up crying."

A few years ago, Marie-Do directed a documentary about oysters for *National Geographic*, most of it shot around Charente. If we needed oysters for Christmas dinner, obviously she was the expert.

"There's only one place to go," she said. "If I can just remember how to get there . . ."

We drove out of Fouras, following the coast toward the open Atlantic. A sharp wind blew off the ocean as we headed southwest. The road ran dead straight alongside a canal, once busy with barge traffic, now largely unused, its lock houses crumbling, the water filmed with algae. Herons stared from the roadside, and on dark ponds, pairs of swans floated in a hopeless beauty. In East Anglia, they called this fen country. If we turned off, we'd be bogged to the axles within a hundred metres.

Crossing the river Seudre, we ignored the shallow white arc of the new bridge linking the mainland to the fashionable holiday island of Île de Ré, and turned south, away from the more popular oyster towns of Oléron and Marennes, following instead the wide river upstream to the village of La Tremblade.

La Tremblade was no tourist haven. A director shooting a horror film about monsters from the deep could well have set his opening sequence here. Tumbledown clapboard restaurants and the stalls of oyster merchants straggled along a stretch of potholed road beside a silent inlet lined with makeshift jetties. On the opposite shore stood a line of fishing cabins, a few of them brightly painted and trim, but most sagging with age. At the oyster stalls, sellers in heavy ankle-length rubber aprons stared, expressionless, as we idled by, and dragged on their cigarettes.

"Is it one of these?" I asked, nodding toward the ramshackle stalls.

"Here? Oh, no."

She stopped the car, got out, and carried on an animated conversation with one of the sellers.

Returning, she nodded toward the flats between us and the Seudre. "They say back over there."

For half an hour, we bumped along rutted roads, past piles of rusted machinery overgrown with weeds, and dank black ponds that looked sure to harbour at least a couple of the "floaters" habitually dredged out of similar waters in TV forensic shows like *CSI*. Any habitation where we might have asked for directions was always on the other side of a canal or, if on our side, barred and bolted.

By four p.m., night was coming down. Just as we were losing hope, a gleaming black SUV cruised across the middle distance, bumping along the hump between two canals. Among the battered Nissan pickups favoured by the locals, it stood out like Gwyneth Paltrow in a tribe of African bushmen.

We reversed and set out in pursuit. The road had no name, just a sign, *VOIE PRIVÉE*, and the symbol for a dead end. But at the point where the canal met the Seudre at an ancient rusted lock, we found an unexpectedly modern building. The 4×4 stood outside, next to a line of Mercedes, Volvos, BMWs, and a semitrailer in the process of being loaded. As we parked, a Porsche purred up. This had to be The Place.

Inside, it buzzed with noise and activity. In one half of the shed, behind heavy plastic curtains, men and women in ankle-length aprons and wellington boots shovelled oysters into long revolving metal drums gushing with water. This cleaned off any weeds or mud. Others sorted and graded the oysters, and packed them into the traditional lidded baskets, woven from wide, paper-thin strips of white wood. On our side of the curtain, filled baskets were piled head-high, tied, labelled, and awaiting shipment. I browsed the addresses. Some of the finest restaurants in the country jostled with some of the best addresses: Cap Ferrat, Neuilly, Deauville.

"Do you see the Elysée there?" Marie-Do asked.

The Elysée Palace on the rue Faubourg Saint-Honoré is the official residence of the president of the French republic.

"They don't advertise it," she said, "but these people have supplied the last three presidents."

Oysters

The expensive cars lined up along the muddy, rutted, unmarked lane said so much about the French. No fuss, no publicity. Just that ability to find their way to the best.

We left with seven dozen of the same oysters which, two days later, would grace the highest table in the nation. Our Christmas lunch was off to a good start.

9

Thank Heaven for Little Girls

Every little breeze
Seems to whisper "Louise".

—LEO ROBIN

At the beginning of Raymond Chandler's *The Big Sleep*, the old general who hires Philip Marlowe to rescue his wilful daughters from the results of their wild lives reflects that "a man who indulges in parenthood for the first time at the age of fifty-four deserves all he gets".

His words returned to me as, a year after arriving in Paris, I climbed the steps of an imposing nineteenth-century clinic in suburban Paris with a pregnant Marie-Dominique. I was a few years shy of fifty-four, but otherwise . . .

The events that followed are still vivid. It helps that we have the whole thing on video. Recording births was a profitable sideline of our Vietnamese anaesthetist.

It was he who advised us not to let our baby be born on the date preferred by our obstetrician.

"This place will be deserted," he confided.

"Some kind of conference?" Marie-Dominique asked.

"What conference? It's Yom Kippur. And I wouldn't recommend the first weekend in November either. It's the start of the ski season."

I thought he was joking. "That matters?"

He looked at me pityingly. Obviously, I was new to France. "It does if you don't want your baby delivered by the gardener."

I'm not sure I would have gone to the trouble of preparing this Christmas dinner and others like it if it weren't for Louise and her cousins. And not only in the narrow sense of needing to provide an event to mark the season, and a frame for the giving of the gifts they expect. Christmas affirms family and tradition, neither of which held much importance for me until I came to France. Now, as I became enmeshed in an elaborate network of homes, ceremonies, and rites of passage, they filled my world.

Raising Louise had been as much an education for

us as for her. If there are advantages to becoming a father in middle age, they lie in the area of knowing when to shut up. My parents kept telling me I "should be outside on a nice day like this" and "why don't you get some exercise?" So staying inside with a book became an act of rebellion. In passing, it made me a writer, not to mention the only Australian who never learned to swim.

By seven, however, Louise—admittedly helped by the fact that most French children spend the two-month summer break at the beach—was an excellent swimmer (and, these days, windsurfer). A few years ago, a friend in Sydney lent us her town house. The roof of the high-rise opposite featured a long, narrow pool where Louise and her mother swam every day. As Marie-Dominique ploughed her laps, Louise swam effortlessly beside her, dipping occasionally below the surface to mirror her movements under water, then rising, easy as a seal, to match her, stroke for stroke. As it never had to me, the great Australian luxury, to be comfortable in one's body, had come to her as a birthright.

Aside from the usual domestic disciplines ("Will you please clean up your room!"), we'd seldom told Louise she had to do anything. What she learned from us, she learned by observation. Which is why, almost from the cradle, she ate what we ate. It accustomed her not only to French and Australian dishes but Indian, Chinese, Thai, and Mexican as well.

At seven, she was already accompanying us to restaurants, where she would order an artichoke vinaigrette and, though her eyes were more or less at the level of her plate, carefully disassemble the vegetable, leaf by leaf, dipping each into the sauce, nibbling off the flesh, and placing it carefully to one side.

This so astonished one American couple that they came over to our table to comment.

"I never saw anything like it in my life," said the man. "That little girl . . ."

Louise looked up at them with polite incomprehension. How else did one eat an artichoke?

At times, her sophistication in food startled even the French. One mother of a school friend, returning her after a visit, said, "I'm sorry that I wasn't able to give Louise the lunch she was hoping for. I asked what she'd like, and she said 'a crab soufflé'."

10

A Dissertation on Roast Pig

This little piggy went to market.
This little piggy stayed home.
This little piggy had roast beef.
But this little piggy had none.
And this little piggy went wee-wee-wee-wee
All the way home.

—TRADITIONAL RHYME

We stored our oysters in the chill stone pavilion in the corner of the garden in Fouras. As the temperature in there never climbed above five degrees, they'd keep as fresh as in any refrigerator, weeping away their excess water in the cold and dark, each salt tear making them that much more succulent.

Having settled the first course didn't reduce concern

about the menu. It just left more time to fret about the rest—the wine, the cheese, the bread, the side dishes, and of course the dessert and the roast.

Next morning, as the sun came up grudgingly on another blustery day, I sat in the kitchen over coffee and jotted down notes.

Choosing the meat was always the biggest problem.

Turkey was a cliché.

Goose was delicious, but some people found it too greasy.

Capon, while large, plump, and juicy, was often tasteless.

Pintade, served at my first French Christmas dinner, had more flavour than any of them; guinea fowl die if raised like chickens in cramped sheds, so every bird is truly free-range. But they're small, which would mean cooking two or three together, and the oven at Richebourg wasn't large.

Well, what law said it had to be a bird? I could choose some other meat.

Not lamb—the *gigot d'agneau* was the standard French Sunday joint. Nothing could make it fit a festive occasion.

Beef was a possibility—but why not pork?

A ham? This was a bridge too far: dangerously radical and American for a French Christmas.

Etablissements

ERNEST RONOT
Chaudronnerie agricole
et Industrielle
ST DIZIER
Haute-Marne

Téléphone 36

Registre de la Chambre de Commerce
de St Dizier
N° 850

However. . . roast suckling pig with crackling. . . apple sauce. . . baked potatoes. . . I could almost taste it.

Even as I thought of this, I knew there would be problems.

In shopping for meat, the French, ignoring the fact that flavour resides mostly in the fat, overwhelmingly prefer the leanest *filet de boeuf* or *côte d'agneau*, from which every fraction of fat has been sliced. Such cuts, lacking fatty lubrication, contract during roasting to juiceless slabs, so butchers wrap them in a thin sheet of pork fat, trussed with string, which you remove before carving.

Why don't they leave the original fat in place? Well, for no particular reason, except that's the way they've done it for centuries—the same reason, in fact, that all pork in France is sold without its skin. And without skin, any attempts at roast pork with apple sauce and the skin bubbled deliciously crisp into crackling were doomed.

Roast pork without crackling doesn't bear thinking about. When Charles Lamb wrote his essay "A Dissertation upon Roast Pig" in 1823, he gave crackling a long and sensuous paragraph all to itself:

> *There is no flavour comparable, I will contend, to that of the crisp, tawny, well-watched, not over-*

*roasted, crackling, as it is well called—the very teeth
are invited to their share of the pleasure at this banquet in overcoming the coy, brittle resistance—with
the adhesive oleaginous—O call it not fat—but an
indefinable sweetness growing up to it—the tender
blossoming of fat—fat cropped in the bud—taken
in the shoot—in the first innocence—the cream and
quintessence of the child-pig's yet pure food—the
lean, no lean, but a kind of animal manna—or,
rather, fat and lean (if it must be so) so blended and
running into each other, that both together make but
one ambrosian result, or common substance.*

Over the years in France, I'd repeatedly confronted
the crackling issue, starting the year I arrived. The
butcher on rue de Seine, just around the corner from
our apartment, stared when I raised the possibility of a
rack of pork chops with the skin still on.

He indicated the neat rolls of deboned pork loin,
parcelled in their added coats of fat. "Pork doesn't have
skin."

"All animals have skin, *Monsieur*," I said.

"Yes, all right. Pigs do have skin. But *our* pork doesn't."

"I see that. Can I order some?"

"Pig *skin*?" He raised his eyebrows. *What sort of a
specimen of an idiot was this?*

"Not *just* skin. A piece of pork with the skin still on it. It's for a *porc rôti a l'anglaise, avec . . .*"

I groped for the French word for "crackling." "Crunch" was *craquer*, so "crunchy" should be *craquant*.

"*. . . peau craquante . . .*" I began.

"*Peau craquante!?*" he hooted. "*Quelle histoire!!*"

I'd forgotten *craquant* can also mean "sexy". Marilyn Monroe was *craquante*—a woman so irresistible she broke you in pieces.

Retreating from the counter, he engaged his boss and the boss's wife in muttered conversation. You could imagine what was being said. To the French, England is synonymous with depravity. The Hellfire Club, Aleister Crowley, Jack the Ripper, the Spice Girls . . .

Occasionally, they glanced in my direction, alert for the facial tics or dribble of drool that would confirm their worst suspicions.

Finally he returned. "Thursday," he said. Then, looking over my shoulder, "Next?"

On Thursday, the young butcher wasn't there, but I spotted his boss.

"*Ah oui,*" he said, "*le porcelet.*"

He went back to the chill room and returned with a carcass the size of a small calf, which he dumped on the block with a thump that shook the shop. By porcine standards, it probably counted as a piglet, but to me it looked enormous. It did, however, still have its skin.

"Now," he demanded, "what is it *exactly* that you want?"

I sensed he would not be surprised if I said, "Just put a rose in its mouth and douse it with Chanel No. 5. My mistress and a couple of friends are waiting in the limousine outside. The donkey will be along later."

Instead, I stabbed a finger at the forequarter. *"Ce morceau là. Entier—avec la peau."*

He rolled his eyes at his wife. *Skin on pork! What next? No wonder their cows are mad.*

But I watched him with a sense of triumph. Each stroke of his cleaver was a blow struck for Anglo-Saxon cuisine. For good sense in the preparation of meat. For crackling.

Encounters like this are a pitfall of cooking in France. Over generations, the chef has become elevated into a figure of power, even myth. The traditional chef's costume of toque and *tablier* is French, as are the tools of the trade: the Sabatier knives, the copper sauté pans, the ferocious professional stoves, hot as forges, at which the junior chefs sweat and labour while the chef marches up and down the line, tasting, rejecting, bullying. The French *expect* a chef to be tyrannical—an invitation that cooks everywhere have been delighted to accept. A chain of London restaurants used to display prominently in its front windows a cartoon of a furious chef booting a patron into the street. As he does so, one waiter explains to another, "He tried to add salt."

In Dublin, I sometimes ate at a restaurant where the chef/owner, though Irish, had trained in France and behaved accordingly. He kept his Rolls-Royce ostentatiously parked outside and declined to put prices on his menu. Any attempt, however justified, to interfere in his running of the restaurant would bring him, red-faced, from the kitchen. On one occasion, a client complained he'd been slightly overcharged. The chef stormed out, snatched the bill, did a quick calculation, then said, "You're right. The addition is incorrect. Please accept tonight's meal with my apologies . . ."

He crumpled the bill and dropped it to the floor.

". . . but," he continued evenly, "I never want to see you in my restaurant again."

Outside France, the media have gone some way to humanising chefs. TV in particular has transformed them into larky performers. British and American TV chefs joke, advise, promote, confess, even indulge in the odd food-fight. Never in France, however, where it would be professional and social suicide for any of them to climb down from the pedestals to which they've been elevated by Michelin or Gault Millau. TV invariably shows them in freshly starched whites, magisterially at work in their professional kitchens, while the reporter stands by in awe, watching the magic being worked.

This has created an adversarial relationship between cuisine and the French media. One programme sends an undercover investigator into fashionable restaurants armed with a miniature camera inside his shirt, which gives a fork's-eye view of the service and the meal while the reporter murmurs a bite-by-bite commentary.

The same impulse undermined an attempt to create a French version of *Ready Steady Cook*, the BBC show in which two rival chefs are given bags of miscellaneous ingredients and challenged to produce a meal in twenty minutes. Not only were serious French chefs uninterested in appearing; the producers also regarded the programme as a chance to mock the pretensions of those who did. They confronted them with largely uncookable ingredients, like a bag of potato chips, an orange, a pig's foot, and a head of garlic. While the cooks struggled to create a meal from these unpromising materials, a perky host circulated among the studio audience, asking them how they thought the competitors were doing.

Aware of our potential problems in getting a suitable piglet for Christmas, Marie-Dominique and I walked next day through an almost empty Fouras to *les halles*.

In summer, the high-roofed glass-and-steel building roared with shoppers and the shouts of merchants selling bread, cheese, meat, fruit, vegetables, wine, honey, spices—the cornucopia of French produce. Through July and August, just outside the wide-open back door leading to the car park, a local fisherman cooked saffron-yellow paella in a broad pan over charcoal, tossing in whatever was best from that day's catch—shrimp, crab, langouste—and ladling it into tinfoil dishes for people who couldn't be bothered to cook lunch.

But this was winter, and the *halles* opened its doors only in the morning, for locals. Three lone sellers had come in that day. One was the largest of the fruit-and-vegetable merchants, with a basic stock of winter cabbage, potatoes, and turnips, and some imported fruit, mostly shipped from Rungis, the central market outside Paris, and priced accordingly.

The other two, fortunately, were people from whom we preferred to buy, even in summer. Madame Clastres rented a small corner stall to sell the produce of her own garden, and M. Mortier, a jovial man with a belly and bushy moustache like Balzac, wasn't simply the only one of the market's three butchers to open in winter, but the best of them at any time. Even on an icy day like this, a queue had formed at his counter—mainly because of his tendency to chat. Each man got a joke, each woman a comment on her hat or dress, each mother a compliment about her child, and everyone the inevitable advice on how to cook what they bought.

"And now, *jeune homme*," he said when it came to my turn. It was a standard gambit, even, as now, when the person was at least ten years younger than me.

"Could you get me a *porcelet de lait* in time for Christmas?"

"*Monsieur*, you know I stand ready to move heaven and earth to please you. Accept my assurance on that. However, at this late date . . ." He pursed his lips. "Just a moment."

He grabbed the phone and made a quick call.

"Should be no problem," he said, slamming it down after a brief conversation. "Can you wait till Sunday?"

That left me just two days to build my Christmas dinner. It was cutting it fine. But did I have a choice?

"Yes. Perfect. But one thing . . ."

"*Oui? J'écoute.*"

"It must have its skin."

"Its *skin*?"

"Yes."

"*Monsieur . . .*"

He cocked his head. I steeled myself for the inevitable argument.

". . . of *course* it will have its skin," he continued. "Who of us does not? Reassure yourself that your piglet will be as well dressed as if by the best tailor in London."

Turning into profile, he made the fluttering hand gestures up and down his body, gestures of a tailor showing off the cut of a suit—or a *torero* admiring his *traje de luces* in a full-length mirror. Unself-consciously sexual, almost feminine, they pointed to the reason for M. Mortier's success. We were none of us customers so much as subjects of seduction.

He winked, as if he knew I'd seen through him.

"Until Sunday . . ." he said.

I'd turned away and taken a couple of steps when he called after me: ". . . when I will also explain to you *exactly* how it should be cooked."

11

All in the Mind

We know what we are, but not what we may be.

—WILLIAM SHAKESPEARE

In his memoirs, Valéry Giscard d'Estaing, president of France from 1974 to 1981, recalled his first encounter with Margaret Thatcher, Britain's prime minister. They met in her suite at the Crillon, Paris's best hotel—obviously so, since General Bogislav von Studnitz, commander of the first German troops to enter the city in 1940, chose to make his headquarters there during the occupation.

Mrs. Thatcher, not for nothing known as the Iron Lady, was all business and, without preamble, launched into a vigorous attack on exchange rates between the pound and the franc.

Giscard d'Estaing listened but not too attentively.

Before him stretched the place de la Concorde, the plaza where Louis XVI and Marie-Antoinette lost their heads—as, in another sense, had Gene Kelly and Leslie Caron a century and a half later, dancing a moonlit pas de deux around its fountains in the movie *An American in Paris.*

Seeing Concorde spread out in the spring sunshine reminded him of the hundreds—even thousands?—of couples who had looked on that view after a night of sexual abandon. Why, he himself . . .

A realisation struck him, and he stared around the suite, recognising it for the first time.

Interrupting the prime minister in full flight, he explained something extraordinary. Not only had he spent his own wedding night in the Crillon, but he had spent it *in this very suite.*

Mrs. Thatcher politely heard him out, then, when he was done, returned to her complaint about the value of the franc. At that moment, Giscard d'Estaing realised what sort of woman he was dealing with: a political animal, so focused that she was immune even to the potent romantic influence of Paris.

One can only think: how sad. "When a man is tired of London," remarked Samuel Johnson, "he is tired of life; for there is in London all that life can afford." It can

be said equally of Paris that not to have seen it through the eyes of love is not to know it at all.

I would have loved Paris no matter when I encountered it; if, for instance, I'd been taken there as a child: attended the *Guignol* puppet shows in the Luxembourg Gardens, ridden the *manège* in the Tuileries, and grabbed for the tassel that in France replaces the brass ring of American carousels.

Stage designer Jo Mielziner, who created the décor for the 1949 Broadway productions of *Death of a Salesman* and *South Pacific*, had told me how he enjoyed just such a childhood. Each afternoon his mother took him walking through Paris with one simple instruction: "Just *look*." Only when he returned home was Jo permitted to write down or draw what he'd seen. "It freed my imagination," he recalled half a century later, the memory still vivid. "It made me really *see* the world."

Not so lucky as Mielziner, I first came to Paris as an adult, in 1970, a new arrival from Australia, poor and ignorant. With my girlfriend of the time, I checked into one of the cheap hotels that, in those days, one could still find in the crowded lanes of the old Latin Quarter, huddling to the Seine, just across the river from Notre-Dame. We looked around the seedy room with its twanging bed, the threadbare carpet, the cigarette-scarred furniture, listened to the rumble of conversation in the café downstairs, and could only think, "How romantic!" What we'd have rejected as squalor in Sydney or New York became aphrodisiac in Paris.

But even as we strolled around the city in the early spring afternoon, relishing the way the golden-green foliage had begun to appear on the chestnut trees of the tiny hidden wedge of place Dauphine, which surrealist André Breton had perceptively christened *le sexe de Paris*—the city's pubic triangle—we both sensed that this would be our last visit together. Paris changes you, alerts you to new experiences, new relationships waiting just around the next corner. Alan Jay Lerner expressed it well in his script for *An American in Paris*. "It never lets you forget anything," Gene Kelly says of the city. "It's too real and too beautiful. It reaches in and opens you wide, and you stay that way."

It's easy to think that one's romantic experience is unique, but Margaret Thatcher was almost alone in not falling under the spell of Paris. In 1965 Woody Allen made his first trip to France as writer on the comedy *What's New Pussycat?*. When he and the film's director, Clive Donner, both fell for the same girl and she couldn't choose between them, the crew, with her agreement, proposed a competition. Whoever produced the most impressive gift would share her bed. Donner purchased a gigantic box of chocolates, but Woody—astonished, one senses, at his audacity in even *imagining* he could win—trumped that with a real American jukebox. In the end, she stood him up for someone she'd just met that day—but if Paris could transform so dry a stick as Woody Allen, it could transform anyone.

Romance played a crucial role in making Paris my permanent home.

Living in Los Angeles in 1989, on the rebound from my separation from Joyce, I'd become friendly with Suzy, a woman in movie management, whose longtime lover, an irascible filmmaker and addict, had recently died. Though he'd treated her with casual contempt in life, she felt bereft without him.

"If only I could be sure that we would be reunited, someday," she sighed, "I think I could go on."

Being Jewish, and thus with no expectation of an afterlife, she was presented with a complex challenge. As a practical executive, however, she put this concept into preproduction and, with me as company, began to audition systems of belief. If one promised reunion with her demon lover after death, she was ready to convert.

We visited card readers and mediums, and a spiritist church in Encino, but none of them offered the reassurance she needed. The last candidate, who lived in the

remote suburb of Commerce, needed subjects to be hyp-
notised as part of some ill-defined project. Suzy didn't
feel like surrendering control of her mind unless somebody she trusted had done so before, so she dispatched
me into that wilderness of twenty-four-hour poker clubs
and used-car lots to check him out.

Joe was a young psychologist who, it turned out,
believed we've all lived before, in other bodies. As part
of his work at a mental hospital, he used hypnosis a lot
and was convinced that, in a trance, people might reveal
those other lives.

Once I understood what he was looking for, I explained frankly that any belief I might have had in this
phenomenon had been extinguished by the regiments of
cocktail waitresses and bus drivers claiming to be reincar-
nations of Napoleon, Cleopatra, and the Queen of Sheba.

"How come," I asked, "mediums always make contact with someone's dead child or their aunt Rose, but
never Napoleon or Cleopatra? Yet it's the souls of the
Napoleons and Cleopatras that always transmigrate.
And why no villains? Did you ever hear of anyone
claiming to channel Bluebeard or Hitler?"

"That's an interesting point," he said soothingly,
no doubt in the same tone he used with patients who
believed their minds were controlled by Neptunians,
which is why they had to wear this tinfoil hat.

"Have you found anyone who did actually remember Christ?" I pressed.

"Not so far. One subject did remember being in heaven though."

"You're joking!"

He handed me a sheaf of handwritten pages, a transcript of her reminiscences. I skimmed the adolescently unformed handwriting.

"... *green lawns ... white robes ... big houses where we slept together ... learning from the Elders ...*"

"This isn't heaven," I said. "It's *college*. I used to teach on a campus just like this."

"That's one point of view," Joe said mildly. "But as long as you're here, why not give it a try?"

I proved to be the perfect subject for hypnosis, able to drift into a trance almost at will—something on which my teachers at school had often commented. Along the way, I did re-experience some startling memories that I'd suppressed. However, Joe never pushed me back any earlier than age nine, let alone into a previous existence. After half a dozen visits, it became clear that I wasn't what he needed.

"But I really appreciate your time, John," he told me. "And I'd like to give you a gift."

As I looked around his threadbare home, preparing diplomatically to refuse, he read my mind.

"I don't mean money. I mean a post-hypnotic gift. Think of the three things that have given you the greatest pleasure in life. Then, as you name each, I'll squeeze your left wrist. And from now on, every time you squeeze that wrist, you'll re-experience the same pleasure."

My choices, nominated while I was still in a trance, astonished me. Not great sex, wild music, drug highs, or roller-coaster rides—just the solitary pleasures of someone who, though usually surrounded by people, felt himself alone.

The first was the pleasure of getting up before the sun, and sitting down in the pre-dawn silence with a cup of coffee to start writing.

The second was the memory of a song, "Finishing the Hat", from Stephen Sondheim's *Sunday in the Park with George*. While the painter Georges Seurat works on his great canvas *Sunday Afternoon on the Island of Grande Jatte*, exulting in his ability to render in tiny points of colour the reality of something as prosaic as a hat, his exasperated mistress is lured away to America by a baker who, though no Seurat, can give her the love and attention she needs. Its relevance to my own situation was obvious.

When he asked for my third choice, my response, again, astonished me. And again, it was connected with Paris.

In a memory so vivid that I felt I'd been physically transported back ten years and across the world, I was standing with Marie-Dominique, the French girl I'd met at the college in Virginia and who had so surprisingly suggested a new way of serving asparagus. Much later, we'd enjoyed a romance, and though it had been over for some years, we'd remained friends.

In my memory, it was a winter's day and we were standing on the edge of the sprawling flea market of Clignancourt, on the outskirts of Paris. We were eating thin French fries with mustard out of a cone of paper. I could taste the salt and oil, see the wind ruffling the fur collar of her coat, feel the cold through my feet. Emotions too complex to analyse lifted me like a wave.

Driving back home in a daze, I rang her in Paris. Wouldn't she like to visit me in Los Angeles? Not long after, she did.

From the moment she got off the plane, we both sensed a fundamental change in our relationship. Like a bottle of wine that only comes into its best after it's had time to breathe, our love was ready to drink.

For the next ten days, we barely spent a minute apart. And in the quiet times, almost without discussing it, we became aware that this part of our lives was coming to a close. We would return to Paris, set up a home, marry, have children.

All in the Mind

Within three weeks, to the astonishment of my friends, I'd emptied my apartment, disposed of my possessions, and booked a flight to Paris, a city where I'd never lived, in a country where I knew nobody, and whose language I couldn't speak. I was fifty, Marie-Dominique ten years younger, and nobody believed it would last a fortnight, if indeed it survived as far as the airport.

12

Apples

Stay me with flagons, comfort me with apples,

for I am sick of love.

—THE SONG OF SOLOMON 2:5

Unless the questioner is also in the same business, anyone a writer meets socially will eventually ask the same
three questions.

The first is "Do you write under your own name?"
I take this to mean "I've never heard of you". Another
author, spikier than me, always responds, "Name some
writers, and I'll tell you if I'm one of them." Invariably,
the questioner can't name *any*, except Dickens, Shakespeare, and Candy Whatsername, the chick who wrote
My Ten Best World Cup Blow-Jobs.

The meaning of the second question—"Do you

make a living at it?"—is also transparent. It can mean only one thing: "If this clown can succeed as a writer, how could *I* fail?"

Arthur Miller, author of *Death of a Salesman* and *The Crucible*, once noticed, while buying a hot dog, that the vendor was an old classmate from high school.

"So whattaya doin' now, Artie?" the man inquired once he'd introduced himself.

Miller explained he'd become a playwright, and a fairly successful one.

"Playwriting," said the hot-dog man. "Yeah. I shoulda gone inta that."

Neither of these two questions, however, is quite as irritating as the third, which is "Where do you get your ideas?"

Why irritating? Because most of us don't *know* where our ideas come from. If we did, we'd spend less time staring at the wall, or surfing the net, or watching lunchtime TV with the excuse that we're resting our eyes or waiting to digest our lunch. The real truth about an idea is, we wake up in the morning, and there it is, like a baby left on our doorstep.

So please don't ask me why, one morning in Sydney in 1966, I woke with the urge to write a science fiction story about an apple.

Not just any old apple, either. The size of a moun-

tain, this one loomed alone and enigmatic on a feature-less plain. A whole community lived in its shadow, the inhabitants quarrying its flesh, tunnelling ever deeper into its bulk, always alert for the murderous creatures, a mutant cross-breeding of man and moth, that infested the empty chambers among the seeds of the core.

"This is a pretty weird story," my editor in London said. And then that inevitable question. "Where did you get the idea?"

I could have attributed inspiration to Ayers Rock, the red stone monolith, called Uluru by the tribal people, which looms above the dead-flat desert of northern Australia. But this comparison only came to me when the story was half-done.

A psychiatrist friend suggested a source for the apple's resident predators. The mothlike female humanoid lurking within the apple, who killed in order to lay her eggs in the corpses of her victims, bore a certain resemblance to my first wife, from whom I was tortuously separating. I could see some sense in that too.

But the real truth was too prosaic to be explained.

I just like apples.

I consume at least four a day. I regularly cook with them: apple crumble, caramelised tarte Tatin, baked apples, cored and stuffed with marmalade, not to mention the stewed apple the French call *compote*. Since coming to France, I'd also learned to use them as a vegetable, dicing and dry-frying them to complement *boudin* veal sausage or preserved duck: *confit de canard*.

From the start, I knew our Christmas porker must have some apple accompaniment. Apple and pork are a perfect match. The tartness of the fruit cuts the greasiness of the meat's fat and lifts the blandness of the lean. But I detested the sugary mush that passes for apple sauce in Anglo-Saxon countries. The best pork deserved the best apple. I just had to decide what it would be.

Of the better apples, my favourites were English. I'd discovered them in my first year there, when my friend Monica and I lived on a shoestring in a tiny unheated cottage on the former estate of Randolph Churchill, son of Sir Winston, at the foot of Cemetery Lane in the Suffolk village of East Bergholt. It had been lent to us by the Australian writer Randolph Stow, who was spending six months as a writer-in-residence in Scandinavia. His generosity was fortuitous, since we were flat broke, with no prospect of employment until I could finish a book and Monica could find a job as schoolteacher.

Ours was the classic situation of "the rich man in his castle, the poor man at his gate". Fishpond Cottage was almost painfully picturesque but situated in one of the worst frost-spots in East Anglia, and completely without heating. We kept the open fire in the living room burning day and night and, since we couldn't afford to buy firewood, fed it with fallen branches gathered along the roadside.

Apple orchards surrounded the village, and we routinely raided them for windfalls. The local slang for this was scrumping. The potent cider home-brewed from such freebies is still called scrumpy.

Those apples were either Bramleys or Cox's Orange Pippins—emblematic, to my mind, of the two social strands of East Bergholt. The Cox, small, sharp, acid, crunchy, had the flashiness of the London yuppies who kept cottages there as weekenders. They drove too fast along our narrow lanes—"more Volvos on these roads today," complained one local, "than squashed hedgehogs"—and parked three-deep around the grocery in nearby Dedham, which boasted of being the Fortnum and Mason of East Anglia.

Randolph Churchill, who'd died the year before we arrived, had been the doyen of this group. A failed politician and erratic author, he grew up disastrously spoiled by his father, Winston, who actually declined a peerage since it would make Randolph a hereditary peer and thus ineligible to stand for parliament. As it turned out, Randolph lacked his father's flair for politics and, after a patchy career, retired to East Bergholt to pursue a life as part-time writer and full-time drunk.

Apples

As his inheritance trickled away, his accountant suggested some economies. He'd concede the need for a butler, maids, housekeeper, gardeners, even the cook—but was it really necessary to employ an additional chef just to bake pastry?

Randolph was appalled. "May'nt a man have a *biscuit*?" he bleated.

If Randolph embodied the Cox's Pippin, the other local apple, the Bramley, large and knobbly, found its human counterpart in Bob Peartree, the amiable handyman we inherited with the cottage, who could be found most afternoons digging at the bottom of the garden or, a little later, dispensing rural wisdom in The Beehive pub.

Bob showed us how to preserve the Bramleys, which, in the season, covered a big tree in our garden. Wrapping each in newspaper, we laid them out, slightly apart, in our little attic. Separated like this, in the cool and dark, with the newspaper conserving the ethylene gas that ripened and preserved them, they survived for months, their starches transmuting into sugar, their water evaporating, so that, by early spring, the skin of the survivors had wrinkled like the faces of old men. Bitten into, the fruit was densely sweet, with an aroma close to perfume.

After a lifetime of munching, topped with this hands-on education in the English countryside, I thought I knew apples—until, one day in Paris a few years ago, our friend Victor, a journalist based in the south, came to stay overnight after a day attending a round of promotional events.

He arrived loaded with giveaways: soaps, shampoos and fragrances, teas, and, of more interest to me, a sack of assorted apples from the French Association of Apple Growers, which had helpfully labelled each one with the variety's name.

I already knew the flaccid Golden Delicious, the slick, enameled Granny Smith, the streaked red Reinette, and the Californian glow of the Pink Lady. But there were a few I'd never seen before—not surprising, since, according to the press handout, the total of all surviving varieties of apple ran into thousands.

Out of curiosity, I tried a Golden Delicious. To my astonishment, it had real flavour.

"Well, do you wonder?" Victor said. "They probably sorted through hundreds to find these. Nothing but the best for the press."

"I wish you could buy them this good in shops."

"I'm sure you can," he said, "at Fauchon or Hediard"—the Paris equivalents of Harrod's or Fortnum and Mason.

• • •

Apples

Standing in the icy market hall in Fouras that winter morning, thinking about the right apple to accompany our pig for Christmas dinner, I wished we had a guide from the French Association of Apple Growers.

As it turned out, there was someone nearby almost as good. Madame Clastres and Bob Peartree would have made a perfect couple. Both were large and a little lopsided, like Bramley apples, but full of humour and good sense.

Every day of the year, *Madame* opened her little stall in the market, a squared-off U-shape just big enough for her to stand in, and to reach the contents of each pannier or box without walking a step. Almost everything came from her garden and orchard; the eggs were from her hens, and any leftover fruit went into the jams that she made herself.

In season, nobody stocked more succulent tomatoes. A supermarket buyer would have turned up his nose at their knobbiness, their folds, their little patches of unripened green, but they remain, particularly when dressed with oil, salt, lemon juice, and *Madame*'s pungent basil and garlic, the most delicious I've ever eaten.

"I didn't expect to see you here, *Madame*," I said.

She shrugged. "One must eat."

Did she mean her or us? Not that it made much difference.

"*Madame*," I said. "An apple . . . for cooking . . ."

She didn't hesitate. From under the counter, she lifted a small box of muddy yellow-brown fruit, flattened, skin spotted with the brown specks one associated with blight or insect damage. If I'd seen such apples lying on the ground of an orchard, I wouldn't have bothered picking them up.

"Clochards," she said.

In French slang, *clochard* means "tramp". In the days when Les Halles, Paris's biggest wholesale produce market, still dominated the centre of the city, the sounding of a bell—or *cloche*—signified that trading was over for the day. Hearing it, the homeless hovering outside surged in to scavenge discarded and overripe fruit and vegetables, stale bread, unsold meat.

Certainly the Clochard deserved its name. If ever an apple looked like a bum, this was it.

"And you recommend them—for a *compote*, say?"

"For any dish. Try them." She filled a bag. "If you don't agree, bring them back."

That night, I pan-fried two pork chops in a little butter, peeled and sliced one of the apples, scattered the pieces over and around the pork, reduced the heat almost to nothing, and put on a lid.

When I lifted it twenty minutes later, a wave of steam carried the odours of fruit and meat through the house. Cooked in their own juices, the chops were succulent and tender. The pieces of apple, far from turning to mush, were translucent and intact. Better still, heat at the bottom of the pan had caramelised their sugar, turning the lower surfaces a rich brown.

Lifting the chops onto a plate, I surrounded them with the apple pieces, deglazed the pan with a little Calvados, tossed in a pinch of salt, and poured the sauce over the dish.

It was the kind of simple cooking France has made its own: local ingredients, bought fresh, prepared quickly and simply, and served with care.

"Some wine?" Marie-Do said.

"You mean Courtepaille left any?" That "broken" case of Margaux still rankled.

"A couple of bottles. Not enough for Christmas, though."

As we sat down to *côtes de porc sauté au Calvados, avec compote de pommes Clochard*—a miniature of the dish I would serve the family in a few days—I felt the familiar anxiety re-establish itself.

This was Friday morning. By the following Tuesday, I would be in the kitchen in Richebourg, as an estimated eighteen people gathered for dinner.

Would the piglet really arrive as promised?

What about a dessert?

And then there was the tricky question of the right wine . . .

As I said, chefs worry. It's one reason for that business's high turnover. According to legend, François Vatel, chef to the Prince de Condé at the time of Louis XIV, greeted news that the seafood had not arrived for a Friday banquet by going home and running on his sword.

Maybe that was a little extreme. But I knew how he felt.

13

Cheese

The cheese stands alone!

—FINAL LINE OF THE CHILDREN'S RHYME "THE FARMER IN THE DELL"

"As we have to wait another two days for our piglet," I suggested to Marie-Dominique over breakfast the day after our visit to the butcher, "we could pick up the cheese."

Even as I said it, I recognized I'd made an error.

The French approach cheese with the reverence the Spanish accord the *corrida*, Americans baseball, and the English their tea. It is not to be "picked up," or grabbed, snatched, or scored, nibbled, scarfed, or snacked on.

At no social occasion in France will you encounter those clichés of Anglo-Saxon party food, the

nut-encrusted cheese ball, the cheddar cube on a tooth-
pick, or the deposit of Philadephia on a cracker.

Nor, at the opposite end of the spectrum, would any
chef confront diners with something I once saw served at
a Hollywood press reception—an entire wheel of Brie,
sliced horizontally, stuffed with fresh raspberries, then
baked. Even to lay eyes on this oozing horror was to feel
one's fillings twinge and one's arteries begin to clog.

Cheese to the French is an absolute, an axiom of cuisine. Correctly experiencing its pleasures requires education, discrimination, even love. Knowing when and
where to eat it, how, with whom, and in what quantity
are matters of gravity, worth a lifetime of effort.

At any business lunch in France, serious discussion
doesn't take place until the end of the meal—"between
the pear and the cheese". Shrewd observers can tell a lot
about a person from the way he handles cheese. Deals
have failed because someone ate the Époisses before the
Brie or gobbled all the blue part of the Roquefort while
leaving the less tasty white.

It's just another damning piece of evidence against
what the French call *la perfide Albion*—perfidious
England—that the British, confronted with a wheel of
Stilton, their equivalent of Roquefort, slice off the top
rind and spoon out the blue heart, leaving latecomers to
struggle along with what remains. Worse, they some-

times pour a glass of port into the hollow, rendering it a soggy mush. *Quelle cochonnerie!* Nor does it surprise them that James Joyce, however long he lived in France, should always have scorned its most nationalist of foods. "A corpse is meat gone bad," he sneered. "Well and what's cheese? Corpse of milk." They forgive him a lot on account of his genius, but not that.

Like the tea thrown into Boston Harbour in 1773, cheese has the potential to transcend mere nourishment. With very little effort, Cheese, the Food, can become Cheese, the Symbol. To Charles de Gaulle, the diversity of French cheese was evidence that France was in robust political health and in no danger of becoming, as some people feared after World War II, a Communist nation. "How can one conceive of a one-party system," he asked, "in a country that has over two hundred varieties of cheese?" It wasn't simply that enthusiasts of Roquefort would never vote for a candidate who espoused Fourme d'Ambert. They were perfectly capable of creating Le Partie des Amis de Roquefort, proposing its most telegenic member for parliament, causing chaos by letting cows loose on the *autoroutes*, and, after spurning the revisionist rhetoric of the Camembert cartel, marching on the Chamber of Deputies, burning the building to the ground to emphasise their point, and probably toasting a Croque Monsieur—a grilled cheese sandwich—in the embers.

Early in my time in France, Victor, our friend who brought the apples, described a ritual re-enacted every August, when he returned to his family home in the mountainous Jura of southeastern France.

"One morning," he explained, "my two boys and I set out to climb the mountain near our house."

He described the steep and rocky track, the pause

at midmorning for a snack and a drink from the clear stream, the continuing ascent.

"And so, at noon," he went on, "we reach the home of my old friend, the goatherd. All year, he lives at the top of the mountain, in his small stone hut, tending his goats."

The goatherd greeted him warmly, just as when Victor was himself a boy and climbed the mountain with his father.

They chatted for a while—"and then," said Victor, "he goes into his hut, and returns with the cheese."

I tried to look impressed.

"He only makes about twenty of these cheeses each year," said Victor, "from the milk of his goats. To be given one is a great honour. We carefully wrap it, and then, after saying goodbye to our friend, we go back down the mountain, arriving at our home as evening falls."

"Wonderful," I said. "And tell me—how is the cheese?"

The look he gave me was filled with pity. What sort of person could ask such a question? In the light of such a ritual, who *cared* about the quality of the cheese? He and his sons had been the beneficiaries of a gesture rich in tradition, in the spirit of France. Edibility was enormously far from the point.

I grew up, like people of Anglo-Saxon extraction, in

the belief that cheese existed in a single form, a soap-solid yellow/white rindless slab called Cheddar.

To suggest the existence of other forms of cheese was clearly heretical. Even when processed Velveeta slices appeared on supermarket shelves, followed by such gooey pastes as Cheez Whiz, our conviction remained unshaken. Mix it or mash it, wrap it in plastic or extrude it from a tube, cheese remained simply cheese, as immutable as water or air. Even when, during the 1960s, different grades of Cheddar began appearing in Australian stores, diffidently labelled as "sharp" or "tasty", our faith in its changelessness remained firm.

And then came blue cheese.

I can remember the moment this newcomer crept timidly into the market: a few foil-wrapped wedges, lurking behind those slabs of Cheddar. Initially, it was stocked only by the most cosmopolitan of delicatessens—or as we, shunning the suspect foreign term, preferred to call them, ham and beef shops.

Who ate this sinister newcomer? Probably those Europeans, who were increasingly turning up in our cities, bringing with them their bizarre conceptions of food.

Salami.

Ravioli.

Smoked salmon.

Cheese

One day, in my local ham and beef shop, I watched the owner, Mr. Schindler, employ a long, razor-sharp knife to shave some specks of mould from a slab of Cheddar. Himself an immigrant, but from the 1930s, he was now so well established that we accepted him as one of us.

"You can't sell that now, can you?" I asked as he replaced the slab in his display case.

"And why not?"

"It's gone off. It's mouldy."

He looked at me pityingly. "All cheese develops mould. We groom them every day. It's natural. What do you think makes blue cheese blue?"

"Don't know." I shrugged. "Never tasted it."

Silently, he unwrapped one of those mysterious wedges, sliced off a sliver, and held it out on the blade of the knife. Machismo demanded that I eat it, though I was fully prepared to spit it out if it tasted as disgusting as it looked.

It was a mild, somewhat too-salty variation on Roquefort. But if the phrase "to melt in one's mouth" has any meaning for me, it was formed in that moment. The fragment disappeared without my being aware of it. Only one other thing evaporated on the tongue in quite that way—the communion wafer that I took dutifully at Sunday mass. But that papery piece of bread left behind nothing, not even the taste of sanctity, whereas the Roquefort bequeathed a flavour anyone who truly relishes cheese will recognise: a breath of the earth.

A few years ago, Charles, an old friend from Australia, passed through Paris.

"I'm going to visit my cousin in Dijon," he said. "I thought I'd take him some cheese. Where's the best place?"

The correct gift for such an occasion was chocolates or flowers, not cheese. No French person takes cheese as a gift, any more than they bring bread or wine. To do so is to suggest that a household didn't have any of these three staples. In her novel *Le Divorce*, Diane Johnson rightly shows a French host offended when his American guests follow the Anglo-Saxon custom of bringing wine. "Did they think we wouldn't offer them a drink?" he growls. You would no more bring food or drink to a French house than arrive at one in America bringing your own plate, knife, and fork.

However, Charles's cousin was Australian, and probably wouldn't mind. So, burying my own sense of *comme il faut*, I took him to the nearest of the three shops of ace *fromager* Roland Barthelemy, on rue de Grenelle, and explained our needs to the white-coated, attentive, almost priestlike *serveur*.

Cheese

"An interesting challenge," said the man, disguising any surprise he might feel at the solecism Charles was about to commit. "Dijon . . . hmmm. Well, obviously the cousin of *Monsieur*"—he bowed politely to Charles—"would be acquainted with the cheeses of his region, so we may exclude those. And if I may ask, *Madame* . . . ?"

"His wife is Swiss," Charles explained.

"Ah, *bien*; then we may also forget Swiss cheeses."

He didn't hide his satisfaction. Cheese turns even the most fervent internationalist into a patriot. When the Dutch mounted an advertising assault on the French market with the slogan THE OTHER COUNTRY FOR CHEESE, the hoots of derision must have been audible in Amsterdam, if not the North Pole.

Disappearing into the *cave*, where the cheeses lay on beds of straw in a precisely calibrated chill, he surfaced with his arms full of small boxes and packets.

The first he opened was a wizened disc the size of a hockey puck, with an exterior resembling elephant hide.

"I'm sure the cousin of *Monsieur* will never have tasted this. Are you by any chance acquainted with the goat cheeses of the lower Pyrenees? No? A pity. The flavor is distinctive. With a glass of Armagnac, after a dinner of pheasant or partridge. Sublime."

Over the next ten minutes, we watched a master at work. Cheeses of every texture, consistency, and odour were produced. Cow's, sheep's, and goat's milk cheeses; cheeses caked in ashes, in crushed black peppercorns, cayenne pepper, or dried thyme, others sporting coats of furry grey mould. Some were so pungent and hard that they recalled the toilet blocks placed in urinals, others so runny that, freed from their wooden boxes, they'd have spread out to cover the entire floor.

"Maybe," Charles muttered nervously, "we should include something more, uh, ordinary? Say, a Camembert?"

I translated this request to the *fromager*.

"But of course."

Selecting a Camembert, he lifted the wooden lid and contemplated its rind, plump and white as the thigh of a nude by Boucher.

"Would this be eaten today or tomorrow?"

"Tomorrow."

"Lunch or dinner?"

"Er, well, dinner."

A supremely educated thumb pressed the upper skin.

"Hmmmm. Not quite . . ."

It took four more cheeses before one of them coaxed a smile of satisfaction.

"By tomorrow evening," said the *fromager*, replacing the lid, "I can assure *Monsieur* this will be *à point*."

Charles reached for his wallet and looked around

for the *caisse*, but we weren't done yet. Since the cheeses were to travel, our helper wrapped each piece separately in aluminium foil, clearly labelled with its name and region, and placed the assortment in a small cane basket. After paying absurdly little, considering the time and expertise expended, we were conducted to the door with thanks for our custom, and hopes that the cousin of *Monsieur* would find the cheeses to his liking.

On the sidewalk, Charles looked back in something like awe.

"Strewth! I've had *girlfriends* who didn't treat me as well as that!"

Remembering the experience with Charles, I had an idea about our own Christmas cheese needs.

"Let's wait," I said to Marie-Dominique, "and go to Barthelemy." After all, it supplied cheese to the president of the republic. And since we had the same oysters as the Élysée, we should have the best cheese. As a clincher, I added, "They always have the best Vacherin."

Marie-Dominique looked up from *Le Monde* and said thoughtfully, "Maybe we can find some Passe Crassanes."

Vacherin is a particular oozing cheese, so liquid it has to be spooned, not cut. Its perfect accompaniment is a pear called Passe Crassane. They come into season for a few weeks in midwinter, their unique character signified by a glob of red wax at the end of each stem.

I sketched out the menu as one of the better restaurants would present it:

Huîtres claires de Marenne
Porc rôti à l'Anglaise
Pommes de terre rôties
Compote de pommes Clochard
Fromage Vacherin
Poires Passe Crassane

Which just left dessert—and, of course, the question of wine.

14

The Grip of the Grape

First you take a drink, then the drink takes a drink,
then the drink takes you.

—F. SCOTT FITZGERALD (PARAPHRASED FROM THE JAPANESE)

If there was an Olympics for drinking, Australians would score gold in every heat.

Most of us are descended from Irish and Scots, both races noted for their ferocious thirst. Add to that, living in a hot, dry country provides an excuse to consume enormous amounts of cold beer. Beer and alcohol in general run like a river through the history of Australia. In 1808, during what came to be called the Rum Rebellion, the then-governor of the colony, William Bligh, notorious for the *Bounty* mutiny, tried to halt the local military's use of alcohol as currency. They came to his house, dragged him from under the bed where he was hiding, threw him in jail, then had him sent back to England.

In the eighteenth and nineteenth centuries, a daily portion of wine, rum, or beer was often counted as part of one's wages, and payday traditionally concluded in a monumental piss-up, slept off in the nearest stables. George Johnston named his second autobiographical novel after a sign often displayed in gin mills of the time: DRUNK FOR A PENNY. DEAD DRUNK FOR TWOPENCE. CLEAN STRAW FOR NOTHING.

In the Australia of my childhood, drinking was the national sport. There were pubs every few blocks, and, particularly after work and on weekends, they roared. Crowds of men spilled out onto the pavement, arguing, shouting, but above all drinking, while in the alleys around, as lookouts, known as cockatoos, kept watch, rings of illegal gamblers gathered for the traditional game of "two-up", betting on whether two copper pennies tossed in the air would fall heads or tails

Governments tried to limit drinking by closing all pubs at six p.m. This simply led to the "six o'clock swill". As closing time approached, men guzzled a few pints, then carried half a dozen more outside to drink in the gutter until they toppled over, insensible.

On Sundays, in deference to the religious lobby, pubs

IL FAUT BATTRE LA...

international, et
c'est un peu ce qui lui a
porté malheur. De Frisco
à Vladivostok, en pas-
sant par Honolulu,
Champagne veut dire jus-
fête, et on croit jus-
qu'aux Nouvelles-Hébri-
des qu'un Français
est un monsieur dont
les valises débordent
de vin mousseux.
Alors, forcément, à
Paris, pour faire un peu
plus original, on s'est
mis à boire des coktails
— une vraie misère—c'est
à croire que l'on a oublié
depuis 1920, les lois les plus
élémentaires de la bouteille
et que tout est fichu. Le
champagne ne serait-il que
d'épicier à l'usage des commu-
nions villageoises ou extra-dry
pour gangsters asruffés ?

Le vin le plus connu du monde
est en somme le plus méconnu. Savez-
vous qu'il compte parmi les plus vieux
crus de France ?

La première vigne champenoise date de
280 ; saint Remy, ayant bu un coup de ce
blanc inégalable, précha aux prêtres de son
diocèse de prendre grand soin de si précieux
vignobles ; les rois comprirent vite qu'un bon
couronnement ne pouvait avoir lieu qu'en liesse
et coururent tous se faire sacrer à Reims, capitale
de la treille — honorer la dive bouteille, n'est-ce pas
encore la meilleure façon de croire à la sainte am-
poule ? — Agnès Sorel, « la dame de Beauté », seule
favorite vénérée par l'histoire, apprit à Charles VII à dé-
jeuner au champagne ; depuis lors, le vin des amoureux
devint celui des grands seigneurs, et fit le tour du monde en
cabinets particuliers et sur les tables des déjeuners diploma-
tiques — on ne fait pas de bons traités sans champagne — et
tous les états-majors du monde comptent nos caves parmi les
plus imbattables ennemis. Depuis Attila, les Champs Catalau-
niques ont sauvé la France ; les armées s'arrêtent devant la
montagne de Reims ; on ne mitraille pas des bouteilles de champagne et... le temps qu'on les vide et ensuite qu'on les cuve, il peut
passer beaucoup d'eau sous les ponts.

Avant d'être casqué d'or, c'est-à-dire avant 1836 et son inventeur,
le chimiste François de Reims, le champagne, celui qu'aimaient
Charles-Quint, Henry VIII et Léon de Médicis, n'était pas champa-
gnisé. Pour dix amateurs de Bourgogne, c'est à peine si vous trouverez un « vrai de vrai » amateur de champagne ; tout le monde en
a bu, mais qui donc a su, pieusement, se promener, en pèlerin-
dégustateur, de la montagne de Reims à la colline d'Avize ? Qui
donc a su apprendre les noms des domaines glorieux : Verzy,
Cramant, Mareuil, etc... ? Allez donc boire, sur place, un rouge
d'Ambonnay ou de Cumières, un rosé de Riceys — et vous m'en
direz des nouvelles. Maintenant rentrés à Paris, nous pourrons aussi
sabler ensemble une classique et bonne bouteille, rafraîchie
sans exagération, dont le bouchon sautera, comme il convient, au
plafond. C'est jeune, c'est frais, ça ne porte jamais à la mélancolie, ça
ne dépasse pas quinze ans, c'est un vin charmant, presqu'un vin de
demoiselle, il pousse gentiment à l'humeur, à la compréhension sou-
riante de la vie, au pacifisme et à la tendresse ; autant de bonheurs
qui ne sont pas à dédaigner.

Je connais aussi un coin — en Champagne, naturellement — où l'on
trouve toujours quelques bouteilles « madérisées », c'est-à-dire
« passées » et qu'il faut bien se garder de boire frappées, mais je
ne vous l'indiquerai pas, ce sont des découvertes que l'on ne doit
qu'à soi-même, une sorte de récompense pour les voyageurs patients et convaincus, ceux qui savent aller de halte en halte, douce-
ment, en amoureux des bonnes et belles choses de ce monde. Je
compte sur votre sens et sur votre goût.

Évidemment, vous trouverez toujours des imbéciles pour vous
répondre qu'ils préfèrent la limonade ; mais demandez-leur, alors, de
vous payer le champagne et invitez-moi. —— L. P. ——

never even opened, but it took more than God to keep a thirsty Australian from his beer. Two legal loopholes gaped. A private club could serve alcohol to its members twenty-four hours a day. And any pub could sell a drink to a "bona fide traveller".

The traveler provision dated from days when sheep and cattle drovers who found themselves more than ten miles from home could demand the stabling of their animals, a meal, and, of course, a drink. Anyone arriving at a pub on Sunday signed a "guest register", claiming they'd travelled ten miles, and the local copper was free to consult it—assuming he wasn't leaning on the bar with a glass in his hand, like everyone else. Because of this law, the roads on Sunday nights were crowded with bona fide travellers who could barely walk, let alone drive. In the 1970s, a young doctor named George Miller, moonlighting as an ambulance driver, attended so many alcohol-drenched crashes that he quit medicine to become a filmmaker. The result was *Mad Max* and *Mad Max II: The Road Warrior*, apocalyptic vision of an Australia ruled by tribes of crazed auto freaks bent on homicide.

But it was the clubs that thrived. Every town soon had its Returned Soldiers League or Rugby League Club, where members could drink day and night. Barely one Rugby Club member in a thousand had kicked a

ball since school, nor had generations of Returned
Soldiers ever fired a shot, but nobody minded that.

At a regional RSL club, I did once meet a genuine vet-
eran of World War II. He spoke with a heavy European
accent—not surprising, since he was a German. In fact,
the army he'd fought for had been the Wehrmacht.

"And the other members of the club don't mind?" I
asked.

"No, they are good blokes. It was all a long time ago.
And you see . . ."

He nodded toward the niche that held pride of place
in all RSL clubs, with a flickering eternal flame, and the
words of the league's motto—LEST WE FORGET.

". . . they are just obeying the club motto."

I blinked. "In what way?"

"Well . . . Like it say, 'Let's we forget.'"

Alcohol permeated my childhood. My parents were far
from heavy drinkers, but, like most Australians, they
routinely socialised with their friends at the pub, leaving my brother and me to wait outside in the car, sometimes for hours. After a few such spells with nothing
but the Austin A4 manual to read, I took to carrying a
few books in the back seat. This inculcated a lifelong
reading habit, so I should be grateful for their neglect,

though my brother was less so. Years later, by then a bank manager, he found himself running a branch near one of our parents' preferred watering holes. When the staff invited him for a beer after work, he suggested this pub.

"As a kid," he explained, "I spent so much time outside the place, I'm curious to see the inside."

When we were adolescents, getting drunk, and persuading a woman to do so as well, was the foundation of social success. Believing no woman would agree to sex while sober, Australian men overwhelmingly reposed their confidence in alcohol—even though, like cannabis (and, for that matter, Viagra), it had no sexually arousing effect at all. Quite the contrary: too much drink induced the humiliating state known as "brewer's droop".

When it came to seduction, a sizable faction favoured gin, but it was expensive and demanded complicated mixers. Chat-ups mainly took place at parties or the beach. Arriving at either with a bottle of Beefeater and a choice of tonic, ginger ale, or bitters (not to mention ice and slices of lime) was not only cumbersome but might be construed as excessively calculating.

This never worried me. I would cheerfully have carried all this equipment in the trunk of my car, and did sometimes turn up at parties with a couple of bottles of champagne on ice in the back seat, just in case. One reason I got on so well with the British novelist Kingsley Amis, when we met in London years later, was our shared respect for a well-mixed drink. Amis never went on a journey of any length without, according to his biographer, "what amounted to a cocktail cabinet; a large straw bag with handles, in which he packed bottles of tequila, gin, vodka and Campari, as well as fruit juices, lemons, tomato juice, cucumber juice, Tabasco, knives, a stirring spoon and glasses . . ."

Since women regarded beer as vulgar, the run-of-the-mill lubricant to Australian seduction was wine—for preference sweet, fizzy, and white, qualities women were believed to favour. In England, the market leader was Babycham, an "alcopop" made from pear juice, but Australians preferred Barossa Pearl.

As I had to thank Mr. Schindler in his delicatessen for introducing me to blue cheese, I owed a debt of gratitude to those vintners who produced Barossa Pearl. They closed the door definitively on the world of beer and opened another on the fascinating world of wine. Launched in 1954, this poor man's champagne was the brainchild of German winemakers who fled Europe before World War II and settled in South Australia's Barossa Valley. A blend of effervescent white wine and fruit juice, marketed in teardrop flagons of clear glass, it transformed wine from the drink of an elite to something accessible and, above all, sexy. Did its makers anticipate its potent effect? Without a doubt. The label featured playful drawings of hearts, birds, musical notes, and bubbles bursting with the word "pop". Above these gaped a dark and inviting cavity, supposedly the entrance to a wine cellar, its pale doors flung wide in welcome.

That Saturday morning before Christmas, we headed south. At Royan, we took the ferry across the choppy gray river Gironde. Our destination was the Médoc, the rich triangle of land between the Gironde and the Atlantic, where the clay laid down over millennia favours the Cabernet Franc and Syrah grapes that make the greatest red wines.

We'd made this drive before, idling down the narrow N216, but always in summer, with the sky a blistering blue, and the vineyards baking in airless heat, their rows of meticulously tended vines, often with the traditional roses planted at the end of each avenue, offering a paradigm of beauty and order.

Winter didn't diminish the order or curb its discipline, but I liked it better. Among the books I'd devoured during those long waits for my parents outside Australian pubs had been Kenneth Grahame's *The Wind in the*

Willows. Repeated reading etched certain passages on my memory: his description of an English winter landscape, for example; it echoed the one through which we drove:

> *It was a cold still afternoon with a hard steely sky overhead, when he slipped out of the warm parlour into the open air. The country lay bare and entirely leafless around him, and he thought that he had never seen so far and so intimately into the insides of things as on that winter day when Nature was deep in her annual slumber and seemed to have kicked the clothes off. . . . He was glad that he liked the country undecorated, hard, and stripped of its finery. He had got down to the bare bones of it, and they were fine and strong and simple.*

Despite the weather, plenty of other people were on the road, probably, like us, stocking up for Christmas. But, to our surprise, few of the small vineyards had opened up their tasting centres. Even in the large villages like Pauillac and Saint-Estèphe, where we were used to visiting half a dozen vineyards and sampling the latest product, gates were locked, with the same bleak message: FERMETURE ANNUELLE—"annual closing".

We both knew why. The French wine business had

taken a battering as supply exceeded demand. Ironically, the primary villain was Australia, which flooded the world's markets with wine that, in addition to being highly drinkable and superbly made, was also far cheaper. More embarrassing still, in blindfold tastings, French wines were bested by Australian, New Zealand, South African, and even—the shame of it!—American vintages. The result was a glut, a "wine lake" that threatened to inundate the country through which we drove. No wonder the vineyards had closed.

Superficially, things seemed to improve as we approached Bordeaux. On the outskirts, every third building was a wine merchant, offering free tastings, vineyard tours, home delivery—anything, so long as you spent some money.

One shop in particular, in a converted Gothic chapel, was doing enormous business, to judge from the cars and tour buses parked outside. On impulse, we pulled in.

The interior was a triumph of marketing. Indirect lighting, and benches and tables worn smooth with centuries of use, created an atmosphere of intimacy and antiquity. The table running down the centre of the shop came from some monastic refectory, though the monks had never seen it as it was now, dense with wine bottles and half-filled glasses.

Everywhere one looked, signs in English and German advertised drinkable collectibles: crystal flutes for champagne, silver coolers, rustic corkscrews made from lengths of gnarled grapevine. A new baby in the family? Why not give a bottle of this year's wine? By the time the child was twenty, it could be worth a fortune. A late Christmas gift? Grab a bottle of champagne—pre-boxed and pre-wrapped (which conveniently disguised just what you were buying).

But the place obviously gave people what they wanted. At the cash desk, the owner was busy shuffling credit cards and stuffing bottles into plastic bags. All around, we saw only happy, flushed faces.

We took a glass—also plastic—and helped ourselves from the nearest bottle. One mouthful was enough. What he was selling at château-bottled prices was the most *ordinaire* of *vins*, no better than you could buy at the *fournisseur* in Fouras, who would fill our litre plastic Evian bottle from stainless-steel barrels marked *ROUGE*, *BLANC*, and *ROSÉ*.

We searched for the *crachoir*—or spit bucket—that indispensable adjunct to all wine tasting. There wasn't one. No wonder everyone looked cheerful. They were swallowing the stuff. And after two or three glasses of even the worst wine, anything tastes good.

Across the crowd of happily tipsy clients, I met the eye

of the proprietor. He smiled ruefully and half-shrugged. *Business is business, my friend. We all have to eat.*

I found the toilet and spat into the sink. Generations of my Australian drinking forebears groaned in their graves at the waste, but I felt no guilt. However marginal my status, I was a Frenchman now.

We drove back to Fouras in gloom. Instead of a dozen bottles of wine, the minimum we'd need for Christmas, our trunk contained four—all we'd been able to find of the 1998 and 2001 vintages widely considered the best.

"We can always find wine," Marie-Do said consolingly. And she was right, of course. A shop in one of the national chains, like Nicolas, would sell us enough good wine for our dinner. But when twenty glasses are being filled and refilled, it helps that each bottle is the same. And the chances of our finding any sort of good wine in that quantity looked increasingly remote.

The return ferry trip across the grey waters of the Gironde, whipped into whitecaps by a freshening gale off the Atlantic, did nothing to improve my mood. Not even a dinner of grilled lobster on a cliff overlooking the river at Royan's premiere seafood restaurant, Le Cardinal des Mers (the Cardinal of the Seas—the nickname for that crimson and magisterial creature), could dispel my gloom. Even as I washed down a butter-drenched gobbet of tender lobster with a glass of crisp Pouilly-Fuissé, I could feel our Christmas dinner slipping out of control.

15

Does Madame Burn?

I prefer to regard a dessert as I would imagine the perfect
woman: subtle, a little bittersweet, not blowsy and extrovert.
Delicately made up, not highly rouged. Holding back, not exposing everything, and, of course, with a flavour that lasts.

—GRAHAM KERR

As the child of a baker and pastry cook, I grew up with
desserts and their mythology.

Long before I came to France, I knew that François
Vatel had been the first to whisk sugar and vanilla into
cream, naming it crème Chantilly after the château of
his master, the Prince de Condé, and that Stéphanie
and Caroline Tatin, French innkeeper sisters during the
early nineteenth century, stumbled on tarte Tatin because they had no oven and had to cook their apple tart

on top of the stove, which caramelised the fruit. (Neither tale was quite true, but never mind; they *sounded* right.)

According to my father, however, it was Australia and not France that led the world in pastry. It was Australian chefs, after all, who invented two of the most famous of all desserts: the Pavlova, in honour of Russian ballerina Anna Pavlova, and peach Melba, named for the Melbourne-born soprano Nellie Melba. (There was even an attempt in the 1960s to create another, in honour of Marlene Dietrich, who was on tour. The chef in a big hotel created the Madame Marlene, based on blue ice cream inspired by her most famous role, as Lola Lola in *The Blue Angel*. A sample was presented to her at a press conference. She accepted it in chill silence and placed it on the floor untasted. Nobody ever referred to it again.)

It would have depressed my father considerably to discover, as I did much later, that the legends of the Pavlova and the peach Melba were false. The Pavlova was created in our part of the world—not in Australia but in New Zealand.

As for Melba, she was born Helen Porter Mitchell in Melbourne and adopted the city's name as her own, but the food items that immortalised her, Melba toast and peach Melba, were invented in Europe. Melba toast was created in 1897, when the singer, the kind of fussy eater one wouldn't want as a dinner guest, claimed not to be able to choke down anything as robust as a sandwich. To make bread more digestible, a chef at the Ritz Hotel in Paris toasted a slice, cut it to half-thickness, and toasted it again.

Credit for the more famous peach Melba goes to Auguste Escoffier, chef at London's Savoy Hotel in the 1890s. Notwithstanding numerous later concoctions of poached fruit, his peach Melba contained no peaches. According to tradition, the nervous Nellie liked ice cream but feared it might harm her vocal cords. Hearing this, Escoffier whipped up a sauce coloured with raspberries

PATISSERIES LÉGÈRES

and redcurrant jelly, and thickened with cornstarch. A scoop of ice cream masked with this gloop resembled a ripe peach, and permitted Melba to scoff all she wanted without risk of chilling her tubes.

An even more melodramatic rumour about her culinary tastes has attached itself to Melba. Supposedly, she believed that her throat could only be opened to its most mellifluous if, just before each performance, she lubricated her vocal cords by fellating someone. Nobody has corroborated this tale, and I tend to doubt it. Imagine the logistics. How could she be sure of having an obligingly erect male always on hand? And imagine the union problems: the theatre is one of the most rigidly organised industries in the world. Was this a job for the Oral and General Workers or the Shirt Lifters and Allied Trades? Or did it count as a performance and thus involve the actors' union, Equity? It was enough to make any honest unionists down their tools.

Despite their traditional association with pastry, the French aren't great eaters of desserts. Since fewer and fewer people cook, particularly in the cities—it's easier to buy food ready-made from a *traiteur*—the standard dinner-party dessert is a *gâteau* or fruit tart, shop-bought, sliced at the table, and served as a preview to coffee, if not actually with it. Rather than the culmination of a meal, it's regarded as a footnote.

But I never gave up on desserts. If anything, I tried to make them at least as important as any other course. Peach Melba held no appeal. However, I did once make Pavlovas for a French Christmas dinner, baking my own meringue shells and filling them with crème Chantilly, passion-fruit pulp, fresh mango, and strawberries. They were a big success, particularly with the kids, who made up half the company that year. For another meal, I did strawberry Bavaroise, a trembling tower of gelatined pink cream netted with trickles of melted chocolate, and for two consecutive years apple crumble—a rare example of a transfer from British cuisine that became a staple of French menus.

However, what I really enjoyed was setting things on fire.

Chefs, like magicians, are ambivalent about ostentation. Audiences enjoy seeing a woman sawed in half, but the professional is more impressed by some elegant sleight of hand, or the disappearance that takes place on the bare and well-lighted stage with the magician in shirtsleeves.

Professional cooks applauded the clever haute-cuisine forgery perpetrated by Los Angeles restaurateurs Mary Sue Milliken and Susan Feniger, who took that supermarket cliché, the Hostess Cupcake, and wittily created a skilful imitation using only the best ingredients: rich French *quatre-quarts* cake, *pépites* of Swiss chocolate, *crème pâtissière*. It was a kitchen card trick, executed with offhand expertise. Likewise, it's a sign of culinary sophistication to have made a pilgrimage to Alain Passard's tiny but elegant restaurant L'Arpège in rue de Grenelle for his *Tomate aux douze saveurs*, a dessert improbably based on a tomato. He poaches it for hours in a syrup flavoured with twelve spices, then serves it in a puddle of its own varnish-colored syrup, with a scoop of white ice cream that looks like it should be vanilla but is instead, disconcertingly, anise.

But while serious cooks respect such improbable desserts, they shy away from the more theatrical old favourites. Few serve the baked Alaska—called by the French *omelette norvégienne*—in which a log of ice cream is coated in soft meringue, baked just long enough to brown the exterior, and served topped with a half-egg-shell filled with flaming brandy. As for the classic *crêpes Suzette*—thin pancakes sautéed at the table with flaming brandy and Grand Marnier—most chefs regard the dish as a parlour trick, and delegate a waiter to warm the sauce over an alcohol flame and ignite the brandy. The few Paris restaurants that keep the dish on their menus are those that most cater to the tourist trade, like the Montparnasse café La Coupole—where also, significantly, anyone who orders a birthday cake has it served at the table with a fizzing sparkler stuck in the middle. The lights are lowered and the whole serving staff assembles around the table to sing *"Joyeux anniversaire"* while the spirits of Vatel, Carême, and Escoffier groan in their graves.

Not me, however. I enjoyed this conjunction of food and flame. Watching the sparks fountain up into the darkened restaurant, it was easy to imagine oneself hunkered down around the tribal campfire, gnawing on a haunch of woolly mammoth, *seignant*, and likely as not with the wool still on it.

Something about fire reignites our atavistic instincts. I never forgot the excitement in a woman's eyes when, in my bachelor days, I'd splashed wine into a pan and the alcohol flamed up, nor the moment when, as I sat with my beautiful teenage soon-to-be wife in the soft Mexican night on a balcony above the bay of Acapulco, the maître d' ignited a ladle of cognac and poured a flaming blue cascade into our café Valentino.

Such theatricality is part of the joy of cooking. Without it, my Christmas dinner wouldn't be complete. The British realised that when they decreed the Christmas pudding should be brought to the table doused in flaming brandy. Lots of brandy, however, is needed to achieve a respectable flame, and there's a temptation to accelerate the process. Jeremy Clarkson has confessed that, as a boy, impatient with the wavering flame created by the brandy, he'd added a few spoonfuls of gasoline.

Jazz saxophonist Lester Young, famous for his idiosyncratic style of speech, would inquire about the culinary skills of a friend's wife by asking, "Does *Madame* burn?"

So, what could *I* burn?

I had the answer the moment I opened my kitchen cupboard and saw my latest toy, a butane gas torch. So far, I'd used it only to brown the cheese on a gratin and crisp up the sugar crust on a *crème brûlée*. But why stop there? In London, at the restaurant of the great Elizabeth David, I'd once eaten a succulent variation on the *crème brûlée*, made with fresh fruit. Perfect for our dinner. Mentally, I pencilled in the last item on our Christmas menu:

Fruits exotiques brûlés à la façon de Elizabeth David.

16

Bread

Our lives shall not be sweated
From birth until life closes;
Hearts starve as well as bodies;
Bread and roses, bread and roses!

—JAMES OPPENHEIM

It was the summer of 1970, a few months after I'd stepped off the boat at Southampton. I was only a month away from Australia and still as ignorant of things European as it was possible to be.

My friend Monica and I were headed for the Venice Film Festival, which I'd persuaded, with some trifling misrepresentation involving headed stationery from my former employer, the Australian Commonwealth Film Unit, to grant me journalistic credentials. Too poor to fly from London to Venice, we bought a Volkswagen Beetle and a tent, and plotted a route overland across Belgium, France, Germany, and Switzerland into Italy.

The evening of our third day on the road, we arrived at Mulhouse, near the point where the frontiers of France, Germany, and Switzerland intersect, and found our way to the campsite. It stood on the outskirts of town, in a park cut by neat canals lined with young trees. Order and good design were everywhere evident—even more so the following day, when a van drove up in the misty morning, loaded with urns of hot coffee and wooden trays of cakes and rolls.

Waiting in line, I stared at the items on sale, recognising none of them. Where were the square white loaves of Australia, their crusts soft and pale, barely tanned by the oven? The squashy dinner rolls dusted with flour? The Lamingtons, cubes of cake soaked in chocolate syrup and rolled in desiccated coconut? The cupcakes topped with vanilla icing and sprinkles? In their place were baguettes and rolls baked a shiny varnish brown. I recognised the curved ones as croissants—but what about these others, just as brown but more square and fat?

I could have asked the vendor, but the people behind me in line seemed unlikely to delay their breakfasts while he furthered my education. Instead, I took a chance and bought a selection on the "one of them and

one of those" principle, carrying them back to our tent, where Monica, with the skill of long experience (having, among other adventures, crossed Iran on a motorbike), was brewing tea over a gas stove.

A few minutes later, I bit into a roll and experienced one of the shocks of my eating life. Running through its centre was a seam of bitter chocolate. Proust can keep his madeleine. To relive those days of European innocence and the sense of a whole continent lying before me, waiting to be claimed, I need only munch on a fresh *pain au chocolat*. The audacious combination of bread and chocolate—that could only be French.

Now, more than thirty years later, I rose on the morning of Sunday before Christmas, before the sun was up, and battled an Arctic wind up boulevard de Deux Ports to the centre of Fouras. Every house I passed was sealed for the winter, the shutters closed and barred. On the town's sole shopping street, the grocery, pharmacy, and *maison de la presse* were just as dark.

Only one shop showed a light—the baker's. The French could dispense with their newspapers, their groceries, their medication, even their wine, but neither snow, nor rain, nor heat, nor gloom of night is permitted to deny them a warm baguette.

It's customary to praise French bread. Even more than cheese and wine, bread represents something central to the French personality. One of the greatest compliments is to say of someone, "He is like good bread." To deny the people bread or undermine its worth is to strike at the very heart of the nation. Until the Industrial Revolution, uprisings in Europe always began in the summer after a poor harvest. As the price of bread rose, the proletariat either raided the granaries or mobbed the palace. When Parisians marched to Versailles in 1789, the spark that ignited the French Revolution, the issue was bread. As they walked, their chant was "We're going to see the baker, the baker's wife, and the little baker's boy".

If the *sans-culottes* expected their rulers to understand their problems, they were complaining to the wrong place. Aristocrats didn't eat much bread and, when they did, preferred soft white rolls or milk- and egg-rich brioche, closer to cake. So it's entirely possible that Marie-Antoinette, not understanding the need of the poor for something simply to fill their bellies, could have imagined they were complaining of a shortage of breakfast baked goods and suggested, *"S'ils n'ont plus de pain, qu'ils mangent de la brioche."* ("If they have no bread, then let them eat cake!") In point of historical fact, she never made the remark. Jean-Jacques Rousseau, with whom the story originated, only ever attributed it to "a great princess", and probably meant an Italian lady of an earlier century. Marie-Antoinette was only ten years of age when he cited it, and still at home in Austria. But as far as the revolutionaries who executed Marie-Antoinette were concerned, if she didn't say "Let them eat cake", she *should* have.

As a baker's son, I was brought up with bread— though nothing like the French baguette, croissant, or *pain au chocolat*. Just as "cheese" signified only those pale, soap-like blocks of Cheddar, "bread" meant only the dome-topped farmhouse and the square sandwich loaf, both made from the whitest of white flour. This was what his customers wanted: dense, doughy loaves, as symmetrical in shape, uniform in texture, and elastic in consistency as a foam-rubber pillow, and just about as tasteless.

One didn't regard bread as something separate anyway. It only existed in relation to its use; like water, which, whether used for washing, drinking, or spraying the garden, was just the same. Beyond "fresh" or "stale", its quality was no more worthy of discussion than the paper in which the sandwich came wrapped or the plate on which it was served.

Between continental Europe and the Anglo-Saxon countries, the position of bread could hardly have been more different. For centuries, bread in France signified the gulf between classes: the higher up the social ladder, the more finely milled your flour, and the whiter your bread. Of someone who had all his success early in life, then fell on hard times, the French say, "He ate his white bread first."

The bread of the French poor, when they had any, was dark and hard, made from wheat mixed with inferior grains like barley or rye. Unscrupulous bakers sometimes adulterated the flour with sand, even cement. In a French comic book of 1918, which uses Africans from the imaginary country of Bamboula as examples of stupidity, a woman asks the village baker, "Do you add sawdust?" When he assures her he doesn't, she says, "Oh, then I don't want it. My husband likes lots of sawdust in his bread."

Bread

To the French, bread is less a food than a character, with a life story and a personality of its own. If I place bread on the table with the crust down, Marie-Dominique automatically turns it right way up; to display its underside is to show disrespect. Her grandparents still followed the practice of cutting a cross on the lower crust of each new loaf—a nod toward the biblical injunction to Adam and Eve: "Thou shalt eat the herb of the field; in the sweat of thy face thou shalt eat bread."

Nor do the French slice bread. The baguette and its larger cousin, the *pain*, are meant to be torn. This facilitates the function for which it's best suited. In Eastern cultures, you congratulate the cook by belching at the end of a meal. In France, you rip off a piece of bread and mop.

Orthodoxy demanded that we detest white bread and praise the stone-ground whole-grain alternative, but my heart wasn't in it. I retained a soft spot for the homogenous white bread of my adolescence. Naturally, I would serve a couple of *pains* at our Christmas dinner—but already I was planning to buy one of the plastic-wrapped loaves of pre-sliced white sandwich bread, which were appearing in supermarkets to cater to the increasing number of Americans in Paris. I wouldn't serve it at the table, but who would notice if I slipped a few slices into the stuffing I served with our piglet? If anything, its soft white texture would blend better than that of the cake-like French equivalent, *pain de mie*— "crumb bread". And a small blow would be struck for the spirit of international cuisine.

17

The Right Way to Walk

At the next peg the Queen turned again, and this time
she said, "Speak in French when you can't think of the
English for a thing, turn out your toes as you walk,
and remember who you are!"

—LEWIS CARROLL

Just before Christmas, seventeen-year-old Louise arrived home with a new notebook, the sort with plastic
pages and pockets for business cards.

"It's for the cards of restaurants and cafés," she explained. "Also my florist. And my *coiffeur.*"

At seventeen, I'd barely understood the concept of a
florist or hairdresser, but Louise is, after all, French, and
parisienne at that, so one makes allowances.

Still, I pursued the question. Pointing to the shelf

where we keep restaurant guides, I said, "You could always look them up."

She dismissed the massed scholarship of Michelin and Gault Millau with one of those shrugs only the French execute successfully, and which, like that *"pouf"* sound of casual contempt, they learn in the cradle.

"But those include *all* cafés and restaurants. This"— she held up her new *cahier*—"is only for *ma griffe*."

Though *griffe* literally translates as "claw", Parisians have redefined it to mean "stamp", "label", or "signature". It describes the pattern of favourite cafés, shops, walks, meeting places, which each of us imposes on the city and which makes it uniquely "our Paris".

A *griffe* is no trivial thing. As surely as a passport, it identifies one as a bona fide resident, with loves, hates, tastes, and prejudices. Arguments can erupt between friends over which *fromager* stocks the best Roquefort, which *chocolatier* the most fragrant *grenache*, whether Mulot or Fournil de Pierre sells the crustiest baguette, and the superiority of a *poissonnier* who includes a free lemon and a bunch of parsley with your filet of *cabillaud*. Even the merits of rival dry cleaners, hardware stores, and supermarkets can trigger bitter fights.

A *griffe*, passionately held, will survive its creators. Numerous guidebooks to "Hemingway's Paris" or "Proust's Paris" acknowledge this with maps recording

EX-LIBRIS

SHAKESPEARE AND COMPANY
SYLVIA BEACH
PARIS

in detail the tracks of their subjects around the city. And what is Dublin's annual "Bloomsday" but a celebration of James Joyce's *griffe*, etched in the progress of Leopold Bloom, Stephen Dedalus, and "stately Buck Mulligan" around their, and Joyce's, onetime home town?

When he was president, François Mitterand used to browse the bookstalls of the *bouquinistes* along the Seine near his home on rue de Bièvre, and eat at a little restaurant on nearby rue Pontoise, called La Marée Verte (The Green Tide), which, for reasons even the present owner doesn't understand—it was like that when he bought it—is decorated in the style of a 1930s ocean liner. Mitterand died in 1996, but locals still speak as if he might at any minute stroll up to a bookseller and leaf through an edition of Rimbaud or ask the restaurateur whether the *os à moelle*, marrow bones, come with *sel de Guérande* and not some dubious commercial substitute. His *griffe* has outlived him.

Our arrondissement, the sixth, which runs from the Seine up the slope of the Left Bank to the Luxembourg Gardens and boulevard du Montparnasse, is crisscrossed with *griffes* worn by the great of three centuries. Tom Paine wrote *The Rights of Man* just a few doors down our street, almost next door to where Sylvia Beach published James Joyce's *Ulysses* at the most famous of all English-language bookshops, Shakespeare and Company.

The Right Way to Walk

Since we live in the building where Sylvia and her companion Adrienne Monnier shared an apartment, the tracks of James Joyce, Scott Fitzgerald, Gertrude Stein, and Ezra Pound wind up our staircase, as do those of Hemingway, who, at the head of his private army, "liberated" the building in 1944—though not before drawing Monnier aside to ask for her reassurance that Sylvia hadn't "collaborated". (Far from it: she'd closed down the shop rather than sell a copy of *Finnegans Wake* to a Nazi officer, and spent most of the war in internment.)

Other countries have their own version of the *griffe*. In his story "The Sex That Does Not Shop", British writer Saki wrote of a man who, about to buy some blotting paper, is stopped by his friend Agatha.

> *"You're surely not buying blotting-paper here?" she exclaimed in an agitated whisper. . . . "Let me take you to Winks and Pinks. They've got such lovely shades of blotting-paper—pearl and heliotrope and momie and crushed . . ."*
>
> *"But I want ordinary white blotting-paper," I said.*
>
> *"Never mind. They know me at Winks and Pinks," she replied inconsequently. Agatha apparently has an idea that blotting-paper is only sold in small quantities to persons of known reputation,*

who may be trusted not to put it to dangerous or
improper uses.

Exaggerated? No Parisian would think so. The
writer Colette, author of *Gigi*, so loved a particular ice-
blue paper, available only from Papeterie Gaubert on
place Dauphine, that she would write on nothing else.
She bought it in such quantities that they sold it to her
by weight, like potatoes. Gaubert is still there, they still
stock the same paper—and yes, it's still only available by
the kilo.

Marie-Dominique is more level-headed than most
when it comes to a *griffe*. But when she tells me "I am
going to the bookshop", she can only mean the small
and independent Librairie de l'Escalier, just around the
corner from us on rue Casimir Delavigne. She would
never look for new books anywhere else and has been
shopping there since she was a teenager.

Likewise, "I'm going to buy some flowers" means a
walk beside the Luxembourg Gardens and along rue de
Vaugirard to the florist on the corner of boulevard Ra-
spail, where the owner will greet her as an old friend,
and say, "We have some of your favourite lilies, Madame
Baxter. They just arrived today. You must have smelled
their perfume."

Both bookshop and florist are part of Marie-

Dominique's *griffe*. So, more weirdly, is Troisfoirien, a cluttered store on boulevard Saint-Michel, which sells nothing but factory overstocks. On Monday, its shelves will be piled with cartons of an obviously inedible Italian vanilla dessert. But on Tuesday, the dessert will have been replaced with Bordeaux, or reams of typing paper, or suspiciously unlabelled stereo equipment, all at give-away prices. Each visit becomes a roll of the dice. The fact that none of her friends have yet discovered the place makes it even more deliciously personal.

In the same way, though restaurants surround us, we mostly take friends to Au Bon Saint-Pourcain, tucked away on rue Servandoni, between the Luxembourg Gardens and the slab-like side wall of Saint-Sulpice church. A single room, with the menu chalked on a board, it represents the essence of French restaurant-ness. As with so many things Parisian, its chic lies in its simplicity—a fact that has made it a mecca for the literati and showbiz people, like Johnny Depp, who has his Paris home just around the corner on rue Ferou, and Juliette Binoche, who has named it as a favourite.

One wall is dominated by a huge photograph of the poet Jacques Prévert, slumped at a pavement café with his old dog, both looking dour, as one would expect of the lyricist of that most poignant of *chansons*, *"Feuilles mortes"*—"Autumn Leaves". On another, a rack holds books by regular clients. Diplomatically, François, the owner, ensures that when a writer makes a reservation, his or her latest title is prominent in the front rank.

But such acceptance takes time. As the food journalist David Litchfield wrote,

> *Do not expect any great warmth from Jean-François at La Palette until you have been around for a year or two, any more than you should assume that a table downstairs at Brasserie Lipp is in any way dependent on how many best-sellers you may have written. As Hemingway discovered, the amount of time you spent there is far more important, even if you only ever consumed beer and potato salad. Be patient, and diligent . . .*

And OK—a few bestsellers wouldn't hurt.

18

The Spice Box of Earth

"Awake, O north wind; and come, thou south; blow upon my
garden, that the spices thereof may flow out."

—THE SONG OF SOLOMON 4:16

"He's too big," Marie-Dominique said.

"They say size doesn't matter."

It was Monday morning. Forty-eight hours remained
until I had to start cooking Christmas dinner. The clock
was ticking.

I nosed the car into the big toll-paying gates at Petit
Clamart, on the outskirts of Paris. We had the road almost to ourselves. With the schools closed, traffic flowed
steadily out of the city as Parisians got a start on Christmas. Back seats were piled with gifts, wine, food.

Some cars had trees tied across their roofs.

Fortunately, we didn't need to find a tree. My mother-in-law's gardener, Ulisse, would have chosen a sapling in the woods, cut and trimmed it, and set it up beside the big open fireplace. And even if we did not yet have any wine, we did have seven dozen oysters, several kilos of apples, potatoes, and other vegetables, and, happily, our piglet.

We'd gone back to the *halles* in Fouras on Sunday morning, to find, to our relief, that M. Mortier had not let us down.

With almost paternal pride, he carried the pink piglet from the cold room and placed it on the chopping block.

"Do I disappoint you, *Monsieur*?"

"Certainly not," I said. "He's delightful." I looked at Marie-Do. "Isn't he?"

She looked doubtful. "How much does he weigh?"

Mortier checked the invoice. "Seven kilos."

Marie-Dominique said, "But don't you think he's a little . . . ?"

"What?"

"Oh, nothing. He's very nice."

"Now as to cooking," said Mortier.

I half-listened to his suggestions, nodding, interjecting the occasional "Yes, yes" and "I'll be sure to remember" and "Wait a minute while I write that down." Like everyone French, he believed there was only one way to do things correctly—the French way.

Mostly, I agreed. But not this Christmas. My family had enjoyed the Pavlova. They'd loved the apple crumble.

We would see how they liked Cajun dry-rubbed pork.

Back in Paris, I carried the piglet upstairs and laid him on the kitchen counter. Scotty, our cat, came to look. He watched for a while, then wandered off. Relationships in France are not made overnight, and he knew this one was doomed to be brief.

Thinking of our potential dinner as "the piglet" seemed crass. As the star of our culinary Christmas, he deserved a name. I considered his expression. It suggested an equable, even philosophical personality. No playboy porker this. If any piggy went to market, it was not he. Nor did I see him going "Wee wee wee wee" all the way home.

Was he the little piggy who had roast beef? Or the one who had none? Could I detect either gluttony or deprivation in that face? Certainly not.

No, his mien was altogether that of an animal satisfied with his lot. Clearly, this was the little piggy who, embracing the observation of the great rationalist Blaise Pascal that "the sole cause of man's unhappiness is that he does not know how to remain quietly in his room", had stayed at home. Which made his christening simple.

"Pascal, *mon vieux*," I said. "I hope we're going to be friends."

I opened my spice cupboard and took stock of the supply. It was more than ample, thanks to a recent stopover in India, in the huge west-coast port of Mumbai, formerly Bombay.

Though India was new to me, I was ready to like it.

There was almost no country whose cuisine I admired more. From the moment Indian food began to appear in Australia in the late 1950s, I'd been its most enthusiastic eater—and, very soon after, cook.

We arrived from Paris on a flight that landed at one a.m. Nothing prepared us for Mumbai's ancient air terminal, a shed the size of an aircraft hangar, seething with mobs of white-shirted men. Some wrestled overloaded trolleys of luggage, with a few imperturbable children invariably perched on top. The others just stood silent, smoking, staring.

Outside, a wave of heat was made even more suffocating by the yellow light of mercury vapour lamps. Somewhere out in the night, beyond the glow, was India, but all we saw of it was a sea of people.

Stuffed into a taxi sagging on a wrecked suspension, we shuddered toward the city, halting with a jolt after only a hundred yards as two men stepped into the road in front of us. They carried a stretcher on which lay, under a white sheet, an obvious corpse. Behind straggled a dozen mourners. The cortege crossed the road, disappeared into the dusty orange murk, and the cab drove on without comment.

By day, the heat diminished marginally, but the crowds seemed larger than ever. In even the busiest Western city, people move with discipline, flowing in an orderly manner along the pavements, pausing at stop signs, seldom colliding, and, when they do, apologizing politely.

In India, the crowd doesn't flow; it boils, seethes, swirls, gathering in pools for no apparent reason, until the flow just as randomly redirects itself down a narrow street with such single-mindedness that one is forced to the wall to escape.

What were these people doing on the street? Only a few of them were dressed for work or carried anything that might suggest a job. The effect of their idleness was unnerving, as if they'd gathered to witness a sporting event and were waiting for the kick-off in a game invisible to us strangers.

Friends who knew Mumbai urged us to visit the old Crawford Market, designed by Lockwood Kipling, father of the writer and poet Rudyard Kipling. We found our way there on the first day and stood across the square, staring.

Nothing prepared us for its oddity. A round tower more suited to a Norman church perched on the roof of a lofty hall somewhere in style between the Alhambra and a British Midlands Corn Exchange. According to our friends, there was a fountain by Lockwood Kipling, somewhere within the complex, while over the entrance, barely visible under the grime and bird droppings, we could still make out his well-meaning reliefs of happy peasants reaping grain.

Such a culturally tone-deaf building could only have been constructed under an administration that, like the British raj, believed in the indisputable correctness of its actions, and the civilising influence of its own language and art. True, almost every Indian still spoke English. And there was no nation where the game of cricket was played more enthusiastically.

But around the market, in a vivid, living denial of the political philosophy that created it, eddied the mob that congregates in every open space in India. All entrances were obscured by a jostling mob of buyers, sellers, porters, beggars, children, and dogs.

As we hesitated, unsure whether to plunge in or flee, a tall, middle-aged Indian gentleman in a once-white dhoti spotted us and headed in our direction.

"Lady and gentleman!"

In England, his resonant baritone would have won him a job as town crier a century earlier. *Six o'clock on a winter's evening and allll's welllll!*

"You wish to visit the market?"

A large brass badge pinned to his chest read OFFICIAL GUIDE. Official, according to whom? It didn't say.

"What is there to see?" I asked cautiously.

"What to *see*?" he boomed in incredulity. He waved

an arm. "Is *everything* to see. Meat market. Animal market. Chicken market. Fruit market. Clothing market."

I had an inspiration. Indian food owes its unique flavours to a mixture of dry spices, different for each dish, called a masala. We in the West often fall back on that one-size-fits-all masala sold as "curry powder", but the serious cook pounds and grinds his or her own, depending on the recipe.

"Spice market?" I inquired.

"Of *course* spice market," said our guide. "Very *excellent* spice market."

Waving us to follow, he plunged into the maelstrom.

"Shouldn't we . . ." I began lamely.

Every book on visiting India gave the same advice: always negotiate a price beforehand. But this only worked if the guides and drivers cooperated, and none did. "Get in," the cab drivers would say, grinning at our naïveté in imagining they hadn't read those same books. "We talk."

To his credit, our guide gave good value. Once I mentioned the fountain, he led us to the core of the market, where Kipling's ornate creation of red sandstone squatted, half-buried in fruit crates and cardboard cartons. In its basins, dry for generations, dogs and children drowsed.

The deeper we were guided into the market complex, the more it seemed like a sunken ship colonised over centuries by sea creatures. Arcades that, under the raj, had been lined with neat merchants' offices were now engulfed in gimcrack stalls. Everywhere matchboard partitions supported toppling shelves, bulging sacks, cages in teetering towers, and people, people, people—their noise, their smell, and yet more noise.

We passed an alley stinking with guano, and raucous with squawks and cocks' crows.

"Bird market," our guide said, unnecessarily, and, at the next, "Drug market."

"Drugs?"

"Many fine Indian drugs. All types. Codeine. Valium . . ."

So he meant medicines. Because of a loophole in the patent laws, thoughtfully kept open by the government, Indian pharmaceutical companies can produce medications without paying the foreign companies that developed them. Mumbai is this industry's capital.

We pressed on to the next alley, shouldering through the mob.

"Snake market," said the guide.

"Snake market?" Marie-Dominique shuddered.

Through high windows, unwashed since Lord Curzon was viceroy, slabs of dusty sunlight fell across the long corridor. Everywhere—in the shadows, at the corner of the eye—one sensed languid movement, the ripple of light on skins that flowed like oil. That narrow space concentrated all India's strangeness. It was the portal to another, and alien, world.

"You like?" asked the guide, sensing my interest. He started to lead us in.

"I don't think so."

The next alley exuded a pungency as strong as the others, but this time not of chicken manure, rotten cabbage, or human sweat. Clove, pepper, cinnamon, and bay stung the nostrils and caught at the back of the throat.

"Spice market," said the guide.

The next hour was an education. Who would have thought there wasn't simply one variety of pepper but dozens? Why had I never seen these giant black cardamom pods the size of beetles, their wrinkled shells hiding clusters of moist, aromatic seeds? Fenugreek, doled out in tiny cellophane packets by Indian grocers in Europe, could be bought here by the kilo. I bent to sniff tubs of vivid yellow turmeric, dusky red paprika, sour-smelling grey-green cumin . . . and chillis! Yellow, black, crimson, purple, each ready to explode like a firecracker in your mouth.

I left with a bulging paper sack. For the fabled spices of India, with which fortunes had been won and over which wars had been fought, and the search for which had powered the discovery of America, I paid less than twenty dollars.

The Spice Box of Earth

This included the fee for our guide, who, as a bonus, led us to some fictitious cousin or nephew who ran up a suitcase-full of silk clothes for Marie-Dominique and Louise in the time it would take in Paris for a *vendeuse* in one of the rue Bonaparte boutiques to even acknowledge their presence.

My elation about the spices lasted until we were about to land in Sydney, and the cabin staff handed out cards demanding that we declare "cereal grains, popping corn, raw nuts, chestnuts, pinecones, birdseed, unidentified seeds" and all herbs and spices, under pain of instant imprisonment.

Oh, well, it had been fun to contemplate the great curries one could have made with my Mumbai purchases. I showed my bag to the customs officer and explained its contents.

"Go to gate seventeen," he said.

To my delight, the officer manning gate 17 was an enormous Sikh, made even more towering by his turban.

I held up my sack. "I bought some dried spices in Mumbai . . ."

A huge grin divided his mass of facial hair. He didn't even bother to look.

"No problem!" he rumbled, and waved me through.

• • •

Now, a year later and on the other side of the world, I took out my mortar. Into it went Indian peppercorns, long and cylindrical, like insect pupae. Once they were crushed to dust with the pestle, I added a poblano chilli, its glossy skin a red so near black it looked burned, and the seeds of three big Mumbai cardamoms. Next, paprika, sugar, dry mustard, and a spoonful of the dust-like salt from the topmost layer of the salt pans at the medieval town of Brouage that its harvesters call *fleur de sel*—the flower of salt.

Two cloves of Provençal garlic lubricated the mix, turning the black powder to a paste. Lastly, a little olive oil bonded it into a gritty sludge that looked like industrial waste but in its fragrance evoked memories of half a dozen different cuisines—Cajun barbecue from the bayous of Louisiana; the chapati-wrapped scoops of dry beef curry Mumbai market sellers call a *franki*; aioli eaten by the slow stream that runs through the village of L'Isle-sur-la-Sorgue, where a tiny mound of raw minced garlic on the edge of the plate, deceptively white and innocent, can burn the tongue like chilli.

As I massaged this granular paste into his skin, Pascal turned from pallid pink to dusky brown. So did my fingers. Soon, as pork is the meat that most resembles human flesh, it became impossible to tell the two apart.

Marie-Dominique wandered into the kitchen.

"Meet Pascal," I said.

She bowed slightly. *"Ravie de faire votre connaissance, M'sieur."* Then to me, "Smells good."

"I think I may say modestly that this will be one of my masterpieces."

"Don't be so sure." She held up a tape measure and ran it along the body. "Sixty-two centimeters."

"So?"

"Mother's oven is sixty centimeters wide. I told you. He's too long."

"We'll work something out."

No meal of this magnitude would fail over a few centimetres of snout. Properly propitiated, our kitchen gods would see to that. The shade of Philip Harben hovered, ready to intervene.

Even before I wrapped Pascal in cling film, the aroma of the marinade was circulating through the house, just as it penetrated the meat.

I hope you appreciate the attention you're getting here, I thought. *Yesterday, you were just another piglet. Today, you're the beneficiary of the cooking traditions of four continents and a thousand years.*

I opened the fridge and cleared a shelf.

You're going in a youngster, I thought as I put him in place, *but you've got to come out a star!*

19

Christmas Eve

'Twas the night before Christmas
When all through the house,
Not a creature was stirring,
Not even a mouse.

—CLEMENT CLARKE MOORE

The sailor's child swims up out of sleep if the wind freshens in the night, and the apple grower's when he senses a touch of frost. But as my father was a baker, I wake every morning at four a.m.

As a boy, I would hear him moving about the house, dressed in his whites, preparing to go to the bakehouse where, after dividing up the pillowy dough that had been "proving" all night, he'd start baking the day's bread.

On Christmas Eve, a lifelong in-built alarm clock woke me as usual at 3:55 a.m. I put on slippers and sweater and walked through the bathroom to the salon that runs the length of our sixth-floor apartment on rue de l'Odéon.

To the east, half a kilometre away over a landscape of roofs, floated Notre-Dame, still flood-lit, as it would remain until the sun rose behind it in one of Paris's theatrical dawns.

Outside the long windows, on the terrace, the box of La Tremblade oysters glimmered on the metal table where, in warm weather, we sometimes ate breakfast, or enjoyed drinks in the afternoon. After three days out of the water, they would be reaching their best.

In the kitchen, I made coffee, buttered some crackers, and turned on the radio.

Like my father, I mostly eat breakfast in the kitchen, standing, the radio tuned low—in my case to the BBC—half-listening to programmes created for professional early-risers: storm warnings for fishermen, stock and grain prices for farmers, and prayers for us all. This is radio stripped back to bare fact, all entertainment sliced away, exposing the bones of information. Listening to the announcer detailing the state of the seas around Britain and Ireland always calms me.

Forties, Cromarty, Forth, Tyne, Dogger,
West or Southwest Five or Six,
increasing Seven, perhaps gale Eight later.
Slight or moderate.
Becoming rough in Forties and Dogger, Fisher,
German Bight.

His litany means as little as the Latin mass I heard a
thousand times as a boy. And as much.

Opening the refrigerator, I removed the plastic-shrouded Pascal. A spicy wave accompanied him, becoming even stronger as, placing his bulk on the kitchen counter, I opened the plastic bag that enclosed him, and peeled back the cling film. The marinade was working, the spices penetrating the flesh, carrying their tang into the very cells of the meat, where it would remain until cooking released it back into the juices.

With my sharpest knife, I made a series of parallel cuts about half an inch apart across the pig's back and ribs, taking care only to penetrate the skin and the thin layer of fat, not the flesh below. The cuts would speed the absorption of the spices. They also prepared the skin to blister and brown into crackling.

There would be sixteen people, fewer than usual, at Christmas dinner this year. Marie-Do's newly married niece Laure would be spending her first married Christmas with her new in-laws. And Uncle Jean-Paul, whose acceptance of me had been so important at that first dinner, was in poor health. He and his wife, Françoise, might not be able to come. On the other hand, we might be joined by their daughter Cecile, who had lost her husband during the year and moved back into the parental home until his chaotic business affairs could be sorted out.

Fortunately, in planning my menu, I didn't face those niggling pre-meal discussions of the "I don't eat . . ."

variety so common in Anglo-Saxon homes. If you're invited to dine with a French family, you're expected to leave your dietary tastes and restrictions at home. I took my lead from the chef in Jean Renoir's film *La Règle du Jeu*, who has to cook for the guests at a large country house party. He shrugs off the demand of one lady that her meals be seasoned with sea salt only.

"I don't mind diets," he tells her servant, "but fads? Forget it."

In *Roughing It*, Mark Twain tells of

> *. . . the traveler who sat down to a table which had nothing on it but a mackerel and a pot of mustard. He asked the landlord if this was all. The landlord said:*
>
> > *"All! Why, thunder and lightning, I should think there was mackerel enough there for six."*
> >
> > *"But I don't like mackerel."*
> >
> > *"Oh—then help yourself to the mustard."*

This is a very French response. If your religion forbids pork, or peanuts send you into shock, there's no point in explaining it to a French hostess. She'll just suggest you might be happier staying home with some Chinese takeaway in front of the TV.

On the other hand, there were expectations.

In fifteen years, the family had come to expect something special at Christmas. Though *politesse* would ensure that not a discouraging word was heard at the table, news of a disaster could spread as swiftly and as fatally as bird flu.

A friend attending a wedding in a remote corner of France was startled when a distant cousin murmured at the post-ceremony *coctel*, "*Terribly* sorry to hear about that *bêtise* with the *beurre nantais* at your niece's First Communion breakfast. Whatever possessed you to use a powdered fish *fumet*?" No wonder some husbands, presenting a new wife to the family, bought everything pre-cooked from the *traiteur* or, in extreme cases, hired a professional chef to produce that crucial first meal.

On the whole, I'd been lucky with cooking in France. I'd never mistaken sugar for salt or had a soufflé fail to rise. Periodically, a bottle of wine is corked, but one learns to open everything beforehand and take a discreet glass before serving it.

But thinking of wine just reminded me that we still had not solved that particular problem. Scouring our cellars and those of friends, we'd accumulated a dozen adequate bottles, but the quality would be alarmingly variable.

"Nobody will notice," Marie-Do said consolingly.

"I will," I said.

Christmas Eve

. . .

I stood in the kitchen, listening to the BBC and drinking my second cup of coffee as the sun came up behind Notre-Dame. Once the markets opened, I'd walk down to rue de Buci for fresh fruit and mascarpone for my—I hoped—dramatic *brûlé*. Since there'd be no time to buy bread on Christmas Day—assuming we could find a good baker open—I'd pick up a few baguettes and freeze them overnight. Then, in the afternoon, a little last-minute shopping for gifts, after which I'd return to prepare the stuffing . . .

And then the phone rang.

20

The Ghost of Christmas Present

Nobody sees Santa Claus, but that is no sign that
there is no Santa Claus. The most real things in the world
are those that neither children nor men can see.

—FRANCIS PHARCELLUS CHURCH

"But it's Christmas!" I protested.

"I wouldn't ask if it wasn't an emergency," Fiona said.

A BBC TV producer and old friend, Fiona had been
sent from London to film a piece about *The Phantom
of the Opera* and wanted to interview me in front of the
building where the story's set: Charles Garnier's flam-
boyantly decorated opera house.

"Why today?"

"Oh, you know: Christmas, ghost stories. And they're
running the film of *Phantom* on Boxing Day."

"On Tuesday I'm cooking Christmas dinner for sixteen. I've got this piglet . . ."

"If you can't help me," she said, her voice cracking, "I don't know what I'm going to do."

"And anyway," I added, "I haven't even seen this version of *The Phantom of the Opera*."

Even as I spoke, I knew this was ridiculous. Freelance journalism taught one to speak with authority on all subjects, whether you knew everything about them or nothing at all. You could always bone up on it before the date. There was only one rule to freelancing: get the gig.

"Wing it," Fiona said decisively. "I just need a short stand-up. We'll cut in some clips from the film."

I hesitated. It went against my nature to turn down work. And I could always do my shopping later.

"All right. Come on round."

She turned up an hour later, trailed by a French cameraman and sound operator, neither looking any happier than I did about working at Christmas. Still, they should have learned, as I had, that unsocial hours came with the territory.

Paris even had a tradition of this. Marcel Proust, since he slept by day, would sometimes summon people in the middle of the night, when he was at his freshest but they were in bed. These included the musicians of the Poulet

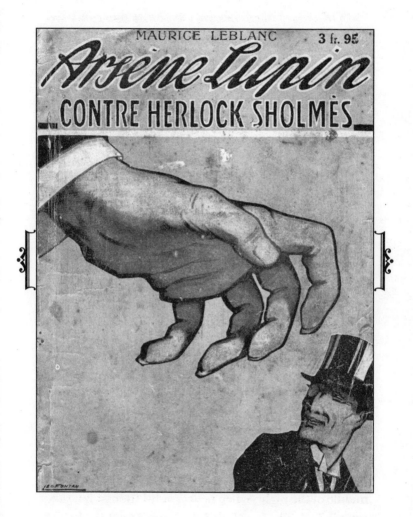

MAURICE LEBLANC

3 fr. 95

Arsène Lupin

CONTRE HERLOCK SHOLMÈS

Quartet, who visited his apartment a number of times in 1916 to refresh his memory of a particular phrase by playing César Franck's Quartet in D.

The musicians came because the money was good, and he provided supper—a dish of heavily *crèmed* and buttered potato purée, fetched by his chauffeur from the kitchens of the Ritz Hotel.

In Alan Bennett's play about these incidents, *102 Boulevard Haussmann*, the viola player comments on the acoustic properties of Proust's cork-lined bedroom.

"We've never sounded so good," he says.

"Especially not at three in the morning," growls the cellist.

Once Fiona and her two-man crew were inside, I looked after them down the stairs.

"No production assistant?"

"*I* was the production assistant," Fiona said. "An hour after we arrived, the director had a call from her boyfriend saying he was leaving her. And she's just found out she's pregnant." She checked her watch. "About now, her train's pulling into Waterloo Station."

"They couldn't discuss it on the phone?"

"Oh, I don't think he comes into her calculations. If I know her, she'll go straight to her shrink or her mother. Can we do this now, while we've got the light?"

The Ghost of Christmas Present

Battling heavy traffic, the cameraman navigated us across the Pont Royal and past I. M. Pei's glass pyramid above the entrance to the Louvre.

Already, shoppers filled the streets. The French might claim to detest the commercialisation of Christmas, but this was the season when department stores and boutiques did their best business. Even crèches were put on a paying basis. In front of the Hôtel de Ville, Paris's town hall, circus tents sheltered a block-long Bethlehem diorama, which people were already lining up in the cold to visit. Going one better, an entrepreneur was also offering, under the questionable title *La Crèche du Vieux Paris*—The Crèche of Old Paris—a Disneyesque reconstruction of Paris in 1491, with four hundred live and "animatronic" actors and a recorded narration by a mid-level movie star. Its relevance to Christmas was obscure, but it was surely only a matter of time before Mickey, Donald, Goofy, and Quasimodo turned up in this version of Bethlehem.

While we waited on the steps of Garnier's gingerbread building, the cameraman set up on a traffic island in the middle of place de l'Opéra, the better to capture its façade, festooned with statuary of showgirl-like nudes. I'd be lucky if audiences even noticed me.

It was an odd setting for a melodrama, but Gaston Leroux, who wrote the original novel, knew how to play on the sensibilities of his readers. Paris—as befits a place where much of what is agreeable, either sexual or digestive, takes place below the belt—is a city of cellars, catacombs, and sewers, sewn together by the sinuous tunnels of its underground railway, *le Métro*. How inventive of Leroux to locate his mutilated hero/villain not in the opera house but beneath it, on a black lake across which his phantom boat glided, carrying the insensible heroine to his stony lair.

Fiona said, "I tried to get permission to film the lake itself, but they wouldn't let us."

"Fiona, sweetheart," I said. "There *is* no lake."

She stared at me. "Tell me you're kidding!"

"Leroux invented it. Before the novel, nobody ever mentioned a lake. The sewers are what he was really thinking of—but who wants to read about some hermit poling himself around on an ocean of *merde*?"

"But the movie. *All* the movies!"

"It's an urban myth. I can tell you exactly how it started. The ground here is swampy. When they sank the foundations in the 1870s, water flooded in. Pumps had to be kept going twenty-four hours a day. Once the building was opened, they shut them off."

She grasped at this straw. "So there *could* be a lake there."

"More likely a couple of damp cellars. I have never

seen such a lake. I don't know anyone who has. There are no drawings or photographs and no reliable descriptions, just some very old and very dubious anecdotes."

Seeing that she was unconvinced, I went on, "The opera management runs tours to almost every corner of the building, but none of them include a visit to a lake. If it really existed, don't you think somebody would have got in by now?"

"Well, if you say so . . ."

I felt like someone who'd just told his child there was no Santa Claus. She wouldn't take my word for it, of course. She'd return to London that night and spend Christmas Eve persuading some film buff or horror writer to swear there really was a lake. And she'd find someone, no doubt about that. *Rule 1: get the gig.*

On the Métro back home—Fiona stayed on with the crew to shoot background—I thought about the urge to believe. The tenacity of the need for something—*anything*—in which to repose one's faith is overwhelming. Even the French Revolution hadn't been able to neutralise that. This helped explain the French attitude toward Christmas, at the same time sacred and profane. Losing your religious faith is like losing a limb. It continues to itch. So, if people chose to believe that a black lake stretched from place de l'Opéra to rue Scribe, that blind fish swam in it, and a malevolent masked figure rowed its waters, plying between his luxurious subterranean apartments and a secret entrance to the stage . . . well, let them.

I had a more pressing appointment—with Pascal.

21

Green Christmas

Angels we have heard on high
Telling us, "Go out and buy."

—TOM LEHRER

It took a while for the French Christmas to win me over.

The hardest changes to accept are those where the familiar coexists with the new: the favourite song with different lyrics, the one-time libidinous lover turned respectable. The French custom of mailing greeting cards after Christmas threw me for a while. Cards seldom arrive before December 25—one friend actually apologised for sending his so early but explained he'd be out of town over the holidays—and the last trickle doesn't subside until mid-January.

I was less perturbed to lose Santa Claus. In France, it's not Santa but Père Noël—Father Christmas—who distributes gifts, and his presence is far less evident. Good riddance to the old coot, his elves, his reindeer, his North Pole toy factory, and, by extension, all those department-store "Daddy Christmases" of my child-hood, sweating in their cotton-wool beards and reeking of BO and furtive beer.

The hand of commerce lies less heavily on a French Christmas than in Anglo-Saxon countries. For this, one can credit the Catholic Church, which allows no festival to stray far from religion. French Easter eggs, for instance, are not brought by a bunny but by the church bells, which, during the period of Lent, when bells are traditionally stilled, fly to Rome, presumably to attend a clangorous convention at which rules for the length of clappers are promulgated, methods of eradicating bats in belfries discussed, and new restrictions voted on the use of recorded chimes. They return for Easter Sunday and, in flagrant defiance of EU directives on food safety and nutrition, scatter chocolates as they pass.

The Church almost managed to keep Père Noël out of Christmas entirely. When my French mother-in-law was a child in the 1920s, she was taught that gifts were provided by someone very different. Every church had

La voiture s'arrêta devant la splendide boutique
du « Père Janvier ».

its crèche. On Christmas morning, the manger, empty
the previous night, was found to have acquired an oc-
cupant, proof that it wasn't Santa Claus who'd come to
town but Baby Jesus—and while he'd brought everyone
a present, he was still, in a well-established Church tradition, making a list, checking it twice; gonna find out
who's naughty and nice.

Christmas in France is less a single event than an

extended celebration that begins around December 22 and, if you play your cards right, can continue until about mid-January. Schools go on holiday until the first week of January, and just as one is thinking of returning to work, the *Réveillon*, or New Year, celebration arrives, offering another two or three days off. It's tacitly understood that family men in particular can use accumulated holidays to bridge the gaps, giving plenty of time for that trip to the Maldives or Disney World. If Paris is empty on Christmas Day, New Year's Day is even more desolate. When the hardier Parisians gather on the Champs-Elysées at midnight to shout their welcome to the New Year, restaurants and shops remain stubbornly shut. The real fun is taking place somewhere else.

Around January 5, France returns slowly to life, but not before the Church gives one last twitch to the festive leash with the celebration of Twelfth Night, January 6. *La fête des rois*—"the feast of the kings"—commemorates the moment when, traditionally, the three wise men, Gaspard, Melchior, and Balthazar, arrived in Bethlehem with gifts of gold, frankincense, and myrrh.

Just after New Year, French cake shops and supermarkets fill with *galettes des Rois*. Resembling flat, round versions of the croissant, and filled with *crème pâtissière*, usually in the almond flavour called frangipane, they come in all sizes, but always accompanied by a golden cardboard crown.

I knew of this custom before I came to France—predictably, through a movie. In Jacques Demy's *Les Parapluies de Cherbourg*, the depressed and pregnant Catherine Deneuve has the golden crown placed on her head by the diamond merchant she's ready to marry to Give Her Child a Name.

Marie-Dominique explained how the ceremony worked. On the Night of the Kings, the family gathered to share a *galette* and drink champagne. A wedge would be cut for each person and one for the "poor man"—the stranger and wayfarer who would have been a common figure in the medieval world.

Baked within the *galette* is a *fève*—literally "lima bean"—usually a small porcelain figurine. Like the sixpence my mother put in her Christmas pudding. Or the coin the Greeks place in the cake they serve each New Year's Eve.

Whoever gets the *fève* presents it to a woman at the table, who becomes the queen. He places the cardboard crown on her head, and she returns the compliment by dropping the *fève* into his glass. Wine is poured over it, and he drinks, to cries of *"Le roi boit!"*

At my first *fête des roi*, I won the *fève*, a tiny

Virgin Mary—ensured by a little kindly probing with the knife on the part of my mother-in-law—and placed the gold crown on Marie-Dominique's head. She really did look radiant—in part because we privately knew that, like Catherine Deneuve in *Parapluies*, she was already pregnant.

The *fève* had clinked into my glass. Champagne was poured over it. People looked at me expectantly.

I hestitated.

There was so much in this quasi-religious ritual of which I disapproved. I could feel resting coldly on my shoulder the dead hand of the Church that I'd rejected in adolescence.

What nonsense it all was! One only had to read a little cultural anthropology to see that every tradition of Christmas and the New Year began with the orgies of the Roman feast of Saturnalia, the human sacrifices of neolithic Scandinavia, the rituals of primitive and superstitious cultures to guarantee the return of warmth and the spring.

Was this the time to make a stand? Should I begin as I meant to go on in my new home, as a model of that rationality and clear thought that the French had done so much to pioneer?

I thought not.

I raised my glass to my new family.

Green Christmas

"Salut."
They toasted me back.
I sipped.
"Le roi boit!" they shouted. The king drinks!
Damn right!

22

A Sense of Place

The places that we have known belong now only to the
little world of space on which we map them for our own
convenience. None of them was ever more than a thin slice,
held between the contiguous impressions that composed our
life at that time; remembrance of a particular form is
but regret for a particular moment; and houses, roads,
avenues are as fugitive, alas, as the years.

—MARCEL PROUST

We got away from Paris late on Christmas Eve, driving toward a western horizon below which the sun had descended half an hour before. Few people were on the road. The main exodus had already taken place, and in a different direction. At this time of year, France's compass pointed south.

The smell of spices from the back seat permeated the car, so that we seemed to trail an alien scent. The simplicity of the countryside underscored the risk I was taking with my menu. The French detested anything spicy and exotic. To serve both was flying in the face of centuries of custom. Who in this countryside we were crossing had ever tasted chilli, even seen a cardamom?

Richebourg for me had become the safest of havens, the scene of our marriage and of numerous *fêtes* thereafter, including more than a dozen Christmas dinners I'd cooked. As we drove through the big gates, I remembered my first Christmas here: the sounds of cars and bikes arriving, the greetings of each new arrival, the exclamations at their contribution to the dinner, and my sense of alienation and exclusion. Now it was my turn to be greeted, Pascal exclaimed over, his colour and scent commented on, the oysters taken outside to spend their last night in the cold. The refrigerator suddenly overflowed with fruit, cheese, vegetables.

Mentally, I checked off the ingredients I'd need for tomorrow's dinner—and stopped at one of the simplest.

"Where's your flour?" I asked my mother-in-law.

"Oh!" She patted both cheeks with her hands, a familiar gesture of panic. "I forgot. I used the last of it yesterday."

"No harm," I said. Plenty of supermarkets stayed

open on Christmas Eve. The village was too small to have one, but there were large ones in Houdan, Maulette, and other neighbouring towns.

"But they'll be jammed," Marie-Do said as we got into the car. "Let's go to Septeuil."

Septeuil was tiny, a cluster of houses hidden in a fold of the hills. We mostly visited it for flea markets, held in the square in front of the engagingly ugly late-nineteenth-century town hall. Its sole *hypermarché* was too small for serious shopping, but even the smallest market had flour.

Le Compliment

The square was almost empty of cars when we arrived, but fortunately the front windows of the market were lit. We crossed the little bridge over the stream that continued on down the valley and stepped into the warmth and light. A single checkout was manned, the lone girl, probably the only unmarried member of staff, sour-faced at having drawn the short straw.

While I looked for flour, Marie-Do wandered off. A minute later, she appeared around the corner of an aisle and grabbed my arm.

"You won't believe this!"

She led me to the wine shelves. The market might not have much in the way of sophisticated ingredients, but they knew what their clients wanted, so these racks were filled.

Bending to the bottom shelf, she held up a bottle with a label I knew well.

Château les Eyquem Margaux 1998.

This was one of the most respected Bordeaux of the Médoc, matured in oak casks, bottled at the château. The last thing one expected to find in this backwater.

"Look at the price!"

The tiny label couldn't *really* say 10.25 euros, surely? In a branch of Nicolas, you would easily pay 50 euros, and half as much again in a restaurant.

"Is there just one bottle?"

"No. Three!"

As we extracted them, the young manager came out through the wide doors that led to the storage area behind the market. Like the server at the counter, he would obviously rather have been somewhere else. But he brightened as he saw us piling wine into our plastic basket.

"Let me help you." He returned with a rolling *chariot*.

"This is a discovery," I said. "We never expected to find a Margaux of this quality in, well . . ."

"No, you're quite right. People here won't pay that for their wine. They prefer this." He waved a hand at the shelves of cheap reds and the two-litre cardboard boxes, which increasingly dominated the market. "I don't suppose I've sold a bottle of this since I put it out more than a year ago. I'll never get rid of the rest."

"The *rest*?"

"There's the best part of a case out back," he said. "Maybe two, even." He looked at us calculatingly. "If you're interested, I could give you a discount."

We drove back to Richebourg in a daze, giggling occasionally at the unexpectedness of acquiring two cases of château-bottled Margaux for less than we'd pay in a restaurant for three bottles. The joke would be on us if the wine has somehow spoiled in storage, but I knew it had not. Wine of this quality was made to last.

It seemed, despite what the French thought, there was *really* a Santa Claus.

The western sky wasn't yet entirely dark, and the giant trees in the garden held their silhouettes against the sky. Their bare limbs were hung with spherical bunches of mistletoe, like tree-caught versions of the tumbleweeds that I'd seen bowl across the road of the high desert between California and Nevada. With its ability to live apparently on air, making no contact with the ground, and to bear, in the heart of winter, tiny fruit that, crushed, exuded a liquid that looked like semen, mistletoe seemed the very paragon of fertility. Women hoping for children surrounded themselves with it in orgiastic rites, the only survival of which is our chaste tradition of "a kiss under the mistletoe".

When one of these trees fell, Ulisse the gardener let it lie until the wood dried out, then cut it up with a chainsaw and piled it in heaps around the garden. Before the light disappeared entirely, I walked down to the nearest of his piles and dragged out some logs for the night, tearing off the vines that had grown over and among them. They'd been cut in the summer, but the tree itself fell many years earlier—eighteen years before, to be exact. I had been here, with Marie-Dominique, in the big bed, listening to the hurricane roar. That night, in this house, Louise had been conceived; Louise whom, looking back through the window into the salon, I could see, now a slim eighteen-year-old with long blond hair, draping tinsel on the Christmas tree.

Proust was right. Any house or garden or town existed only as the sum of the feelings experienced there. It was remembering history and maintaining tradition that kept the material world alive.

23

Project Piglet

The pig an unclean animal? Why, the pig is the
cleanest animal there is. Except for my father, of course.

—GROUCHO MARX

"He's too long!"

"I told you," Marie-Do said.

Pascal lay across the largest baking dish in the house. Even placed diagonally, his snout overhung one corner and his tail the other.

"We could cut off the head," she suggested.

"No!"

The very thought was repellent. To present a decapitated porker would be an admission of defeat—not to mention a tactless reminder of the days of the guillotine.

I should have listened to M. Mortier's cooking advice—though it probably didn't cover this problem. I turned over his carcass and peered into the interior, not yet packed with stuffing. But I was disappointed: there was no solution written on the inside, a porcine *mode d'emploi*, or user's guide.

Only one solution presented itself.

Whom can we ring up?

We had a history of Christmas-morning phone calls. One year, I'd made fruit mince tarts, which, though they tasted fine, lacked the satisfying crunch I remembered from childhood—a deficiency we narrowed down to the lack of the translucent glaze that my father used to coat the marinated raisins and candied peel.

As it was still early evening in Australia, I'd rung my father in Sydney.

"OK," he said when I explained the problem, "take some icing sugar . . ."

He spent ten expensive long-distance minutes walking me through the technique of glazing mince tarts. It made each of them worth about $25. But they *were* delicious.

"Ring up whom, exactly?" Marie-Dominique asked.

"Where's Jean-Pierre at the moment?"

"Jean-Pierre? At home, I expect."

"Do you have his number?"

"Yes. Why? He can't boil an egg. Marie-Christine does all the cooking."

"But he's a surgeon."

"So?"

"This is a surgical problem."

Fortunately, Jean-Pierre was already out of bed. No parent sleeps in on Christmas morning.

"OK, I get it," he said before I'd half-explained my problem. "Do you have a scalpel—I mean, a sharp knife? Not one of those *Psycho* things. Something about the length of a table knife but with a good point."

He stopped, and said off-phone, "Not now, darling. Daddy's working. I'll show you how to put it together in a minute."

Back on line, he continued, "Got it? Right. Turn the patient . . . er, pig over. See where the large vertebrae at the front change size and become the smaller ones of the spine? Push the point of the knife in behind the last of the big ones, and separate it from the first of the smaller."

I did. The point went in with surprising ease.

"Yes."

"Keep cutting until you're through the cartilage. You'll feel the lessening of pressure. Then take out the knife, and break the spine."

"How?"

"Well, I wouldn't admit this to anyone else, but in the operating room we just put the patient over the edge of the table and give him a whack."

I placed Pascal's back against the edge of the work surface—*Sorry about this, old chap*—braced the head end with one hand and pushed down with the other. There was the kind of crack one never wants to hear from one's own body. Abruptly, his formerly pliable body sagged.

Turning him over and looking inside, I saw the spinal column visibly gaping at the point where I'd inserted the knife. It created a hinge. If I cut through the flesh between two of the ribs on either side, he would fold back on himself, snout almost touching his tail—a perfect size for the oven.

"You're a genius," I said.

"Congratulations," Jean-Pierre said. "You've just performed intervertebral separation of the lumbar spine. Without anaesthesia, admittedly, and without a medical licence, but still, a considerable achievement. My fee for assisting at a procedure like this would be five thousand euros, but it's Christmas, so let's make it three thousand. My bill will be in the mail. Now if you excuse me, I have to help my five-year-old assemble her SuperHetrodyne TV Learning System. Nothing I do seems to make it work."

This was something I knew about.

"I'll give you a diagnosis for free. Batteries aren't included."

"What do you mean there are no batteries? There must be batteries!"

"None. Believe me. There never are with that sort of toy."

"Really? But that's absurd! What am I supposed to do, on Christmas Day?"

At last! The line I'd been waiting all my life to say to a doctor. "Take two aspirin," I said, "and call me in the morning."

• • •

I rubbed the dark and fragrant skin of the now hairpin-shaped Pascal inside and outside with olive oil, and arranged him on the oven's rack, with a deep baking dish on the shelf below to catch the fat and drippings. He would roast more evenly that way.

"What about the stuffing?" Marie-Do asked.

"No problem. We'll cook it separately."

Earlier, I'd mixed the soft American (ssshhh!) bread crumbs with chopped apple, celery—including some of its leaves—fresh sage and marjoram, onions, and seasonings, including a few flakes of dried chilli. Oiling a sheet of foil, I shaped the stuffing into a cylinder, leaving it to be put in the oven for the last hour of cooking.

With Pascal safely roasting, we could peel the potatoes and drop them into salted cold water for later parboiling. Nothing guarantees a crunchy exterior more than five minutes of boiling before they go into the oven.

"Potatoes and pork," Marie-Do said. "Is that enough?"

"With oysters, cheese, pears, and dessert? Should be. You think we need another vegetable?"

"Well, Jean-Paul's teeth . . . He can't chew very well."

"I thought he and Françoise . . ."

"No, they'll be here. Word has got around that you're preparing something special."

"What do we have?"

Except for what we'd brought from Paris, my mother-in-law's fridge and cupboards were mostly bare. She spent less time here in winter and didn't stock up. In the vegetable crisper, however, a dozen deprived-looking carrots huddled.

Carrot pudding!

I peeled the carrots, boiled them soft, and put them in the food processor—called a *robot* by the French, who hate using anyone else's word for an appliance—with an egg, some flour, cumin and cinnamon, salt and pepper. Into the mix also went a tub of cottage cheese, about to pass its sell-by date, which I found lurking at the back of the fridge. Whizzing them up produced an orange-coloured purée, which I piled into a buttered dish. It could go into the oven at the same time as the potatoes and stuffing.

"Where did you find that recipe?" Marie-Do asked.

"I didn't. I ate it once somewhere and figured out what it contained. Works with sweet potatoes too. Probably parsnips as well." In my mind, I sent a silent prayer to the shade of Philip Harben.

In the oven, Pascal had begun to look less raw,

though he still had two hours or more to go. Knocking the top off a bottle of Guinness stout, I poured it, foaming, over him. The malt flavour and the sugar would cling to the skin, while the liquid vaporised, keeping the meat moist.

Next, we unwrapped the Vacherin, chosen by the *fromager* at Barthelemy to be *à point* for today's meal. The upper crust, smooth and firm when immature, had rippled into deep corrugations, spongy to the touch. At room temperature, the cheese underneath would be so deliquescent that, without the wooden surround, it would ooze into a puddle.

Peeling the Passe Crassane pears that went with it could wait until the last minute.

Which left dessert.

"You still won't tell me what you're making?" Marie-Do asked.

"It's a surprise."

"Surprises are an enthusiasm of young societies," she said pedantically. "The French don't care for them."

"All right, I'll tell you."

I explained about the *fruits brûlés*.

"There's a price for this information," I said. "You have to help with the fruit."

For half an hour we peeled and diced mangos, kiwis, and bananas, added strawberries, passion-fruit pulp, and grated lime rind, all of which went in the fridge, along with the Clochard apples for the compote, peeled, cut in eighths, and floating in water to stop them going brown.

Outside, it was turning into the bright, clear winter day of a Christmas card, the sky a cloudless blue, against which the bare trees appeared pasted, sharp as cutouts. Smoke curled from the chimney of the house next door, occupied by Françoise and Jean-Paul.

In our house, Claudine and the other family members remained asleep, or at least in bed. Louise and her cousin Alice were awake, however, and gossiping. I could hear the jangle of pop music from the room they shared.

Christmas was coming along just fine.

24

Simple Gifts

And so we beat on, boats against the current,
borne back ceaselessly into the past.
—F. SCOTT FITZGERALD

By noon of Christmas day, the house had come to life. Louise and Alice, after having looted the refrigerator of juice and Evian—drinking both out of the bottle, naturally, and leaving the fridge door open—had retreated to the clothing-scattered cave of their bedroom for more gossip and even louder music.

The rest of the family wandered down, exchanged cheek kisses and *"Bonne fête"*s, poured coffee from the electric percolator—the house's lone concession to American technology—and took it, with some crispbread, to the salon, where they sat and looked out on the garden in morning sunshine.

These movements mostly passed me by. I was more interested in getting people out from underfoot. A cook must control his space totally, from the state of the floor to the sharpness of his knives. Years of working in tiny kitchens had instilled the habit of cleaning up as I went along. Any dirty dish or utensil instantly went into the dishwasher, which hadn't stopped running since eight a.m.

In the oven, Pascal was looking good. Two more bottles of Guinness, as well as frequent basting and turning, had created a deep brown exterior, glistening with fat, and in a few places starting to bubble in the telltale texture of crackling. Cooking had also shrunk him, the hairpin shape relaxing into a curve, which, I was confident, would straighten out for serving.

I plopped my parboiled potatoes into the baking pan, now an inch deep in fat, with a lower stratum of meat juices that would provide the foundation of our gravy. The roll of stuffing and the carrot pudding went on the shelf below. Almost everything was now well on its way, except the dessert—which, if all went well, I would complete at the table, in flames.

What seemed only a few minutes after they got up, the family was filing past the kitchen door, fully dressed.

"We're going to mass," Marie-Dominique said. "Back soon."

The cook was blessed by being given a free pass to avoid mass. Not that the modern French service, through which most priests cantered in less than twenty minutes, approached the torment of masses during my childhood. Those dragged on more than an hour and were celebrated in Latin, punctuated with a sermon, collections, and a shuffling procession of communicants, all to music of droning tedium.

Alone in the house, and waiting for the potatoes to boil, I walked into the living room.

I'd already opened six bottles of our newly acquired Margaux and placed them on the stone mantel above the open fire. Now I poured half a glass and gave the wine a serious tasting. It didn't disappoint.

I hadn't always liked wine. Good wine demands education. In George Orwell's dystopic *1984*, Winston Smith, a rebel in a world dominated by tyrannical Big Brother, encounters a secret society that claims to protect a few surviving pleasures. One of these is wine, and for the first time Smith is able to taste something that years of imagination have invested with a mystical value. But the wine, which he imagines would taste sweet, like blackberry jam, and give an instant rush of alcohol, does neither, and he doesn't even finish the glass.

People drinking wine for the first time often react in the same way. I did myself. Red wine in particular is tart and doesn't satisfy your thirst. The tannin can even leave the tongue and mouth feeling dry and slightly puckered. Nor is there an instant rush of alcohol.

All the same, you finish the glass, and maybe take a second. And stealthily the effect takes hold. The food you eat begins to taste better, as if the wine has alerted your palate to new flavours. Cheese, for instance, takes on an entirely different character when drunk with a glass of Bordeaux, and yet another with a sweet wine like port.

Before long, the drinker becomes more adventurous. You could guess that pheasant or partridge would taste better washed down with Burgundy, but *lobster*? And who first discovered that sweet cold Sauternes bonds magically with foie gras? Or an astringent sherry is the perfect accompaniment to thin slices of salty dried ham?

Winston Smith's error was in stopping too soon. One glass just won't do it. But a thousand is never enough.

Now that the house was empty, I brought down my own presents, distributing them among the piles, each arranged around a shoe belonging to the recipient—a vestige of the tradition in which a clog was placed by the chimney to receive what in those days would have been a single emblematic gift.

The lavishness of our modern Christmas obscures how minor a role gifts traditionally played in the celebration. In Dickens's day, food and good works mattered far more. Scrooge, when he sees the error of his ways, doesn't buy presents but gives money to a charity that helps the poor and sends a turkey to his clerk Bob Cratchit, whose wages he raises and family he helps.

Gifts were symbolic—sometimes just an imported orange or clementine, luxuries in midwinter. British comic books of the 1950s, like the *Beano* and *Chatterbox*, often showed Christmas stockings containing a pineapple. In

Australia, where we were knee-deep in tropical fruit, any kid given a pineapple for Christmas would take it as a dire insult. Not so in Europe. In France, fresh pineapples didn't appear until the 1960s, when they began to trickle in from Africa, often brought by Senegalese *émigrés* who sold them from blankets spread on the Paris pavements.

Simple gifts . . . but the modern Christmas had all but removed simplicity from the process.

It's not that there was anything in particular wrong with the commercialising of Christmas. Any pretext for being kind and loving to those around us can't be bad— and how better to show that kindness and love than by lavishing them with gifts?

I even enjoyed the game of deciding on gifts sufficiently munificent and at the same time so unexpected that they would assert themselves in the flood of soaps, perfumes, scarves, ties, diaries, and assorted gadgetry.

This year, I believed I'd chosen well. Every husband keeps his conjugal radar tuned through December to those little hints that wives drop. But, as John Updike remarked, "an expected gift is not worth giving". So one needed to be just as attentive to any spontaneous expressions of enthusiasm that might suggest a more surprising present.

This was why Marie-Do would receive a GPS satellite location unit for her car. She'd noticed one in a taxi, and the driver, as we paused at a light, had been only too glad to lecture us, not only on its usefulness in navigating around Paris but—and this was the clincher—its deeper significance in a philosophical appreciation of the glories of France.

"You will observe, *chère Madame*," he said, "that this particular machine even shows those streets where trees line the route."

The traffic light was green now. A chorus of honks began behind us.

"As you can imagine," he continued, oblivious, "I often used to regard a drive in the country with my wife as a chore. But I think it was Monet who commented, 'The clear French landscape is as pure as a verse of Racine.'"

"Wasn't it Cézanne?" I said.

"Really? I was sure . . ."

Behind us, a furious voice yelled, "For God's sake, get ON!"

After this, I felt fairly safe in choosing a similar unit as a gift. On the other hand, one could never be entirely sure. All sorts of implicit rules govern the giving of gifts in France—like that prohibition of bringing food and wine to a dinner party. Early in our relationship, I suggested to Marie-Do that we give her mother a Waterpik—one of those toothbrushes that operate with high-pressure water.

"Oh, no," she said instantly. "That would not be *convenable*."

"*Convenable*? Appropriate? How 'not appropriate'?"

"Well, it's too . . . intimate."

"But what about those silk pyjamas we bought for her birthday? They're pretty intimate, surely?"

She looked at me in genuine surprise. "Pyjamas? Oh, no. Not at all."

It came down, as it turned out, to a question of bodily functions. Clothing, even underwear, was permissible, as were perfumes, creams, soaps, and cosmetics, because they were used only on the outside. With anything that trespassed inside the body, you were on dangerous ground.

The standard prohibition on bringing gifts of food and wine didn't apply at Christmas, which was just as well for my in-laws. They knew that, when it came to a present for me, they could always fall back on some rare delicacy. From the look of the parcels already clustered around my shoe, I'd be receiving the usual assortment of exotic edibles acquired on holidays at the ends of the earth. ("Oh, look! Jellied yak testicles. I'd get that for John.")

But even in the area of kitchen-alia, pitfalls existed. While people had presented me with enough ladles, forks, pots, and corkscrews to furnish a dozen kitchens,

I never once received a knife. I commented on this once to Marie-Do.

"Naturally. Nobody would ever give you a *knife*."

"Why not?"

"It's bad luck."

"A kitchen knife? I've got a dozen. What's bad luck about that?"

"Well, it just *is*. It's thought that it might cut the link between friends."

It was useless to argue this on grounds of logic. The French are rational people. Unfortunately, this means that once they embrace a crackpot idea, it assumes the same status as incontrovertible fact. (Later, I found that this custom is even followed in other parts of the world, including the United States, where it's permissible to accept the knife if you offer the giver a coin in return—which, to me, simply adds another layer of irrationality.)

I was mulling this over when a car pulled into the drive. The family was back from church. Time to return to the kitchen, to Pascal, and to the gift I was offering to my family—dinner.

25

Getting It Together

God is in the details.

—LUDWIG MIES VAN DER ROHE

It was time to set the table—fortunately another job from which the chef was excused.

Various thumps and rumbles from upstairs signalled that an extra leaf for the dining-room table was being manoeuvred out of the combined spare bedroom and storeroom at the far end of the house and down the narrow stairs.

The Christmas tablecloth was extracted from the linen press. Marie-Do and I bought it at a *brocante* somewhere in the Dordogne, under a baking midsummer sun. I vividly recalled the sweat trickling down my spine as I bargained over the three-metre length of heavy linen, hand-embroidered at its four corners with the intricate initials of the wealthy local bourgeois.

A few stains from its earlier use had given me some negotiating room with the seller.

"But look, *cher Monsieur*," I protested, "at this appalling damage. I'll never get that out." (While knowing very well that modern dry cleaning would remove almost anything.)

We settled on ten euros, and I lugged away, for the cost of a sandwich and a beer, a length of linen redolent of turtle soup, grouse, baron of beef, *sauce Béarnaise*, Burgundy, cognac, and Havana cigars—a relic of the days of great dinners, which, just for today, had been restored, for a single meal, to its rightful place.

The silverware was my mother-in-law's, inherited from her mother on the day of her wedding. Now she supervised as her daughters and granddaughters set it out. Occasionally, she'd swoop on a fork or a glass, tut-tut at its cleanliness, or lack of it, and put it aside.

Once the table was arranged to her satisfaction, she set the girls to distributing the traditional "nibbles". Ritual dictated these as well. Small bowls were filled with the mixed nuts, sultanas, and raisins called *mendiants*—beggars—because their brown and beige colours echoed those of the robes worn by the orders of monks, like Franciscans and Capuchins, who relied on charity.

Another dish held Algerian dates— not the *dattes con-fites* I knew from my childhood, moist and gluey with sugar, but dried dates, their flesh mildly sweet and floury inside a papery skin, and still attached to the stalk.

Dates attached to the stalk presumably taste no different from those sold loose, but stalks and stems preoccupy the French at Christmas. Late in December, markets flood with small, hard, acid clementines from Corsica. Picked before fully ripe, each bears a cluster of dark leaves. Marie-Dominique would have us trudging from one *fruitière* to the next until she found fruit with the most securely attached stems and leaves. As with

most French Christmas rituals, one assumes a religious reason. A reminder of the olive branch brought back by the dove to reassure Noah that the flood was receding? Or comfort to a medieval society that, however bitter the winter, summer and the harvest would return? Nobody seems to know.

Back in the kitchen, I began to marshal my serving platters. None was as elegant as the porcelain and crystal now laid on the table, but each was just as precious to me.

Fortunately, almost nothing usable is ever thrown out in France. Every weekend when the weather allows, *brocantes*—sometimes called *grands balais*, big sweep-outs, or *vides greniers*, attic-emptiers—appear all over France, on city streets, in village squares, in fields and car parks.

Some sellers are professionals touting overpriced and dubious antiques, but the majority are amateurs who scour house sales and auctions for their stock. And no stall, however small, lacks a few items of kitchenware. No wooden spoon is too worn, no pot too dented, no grater too rusted, no fork too bent.

One has only to pick up a knife worn to the sharpness and thinness of a razor blade or heft a fish kettle whose interior is encrusted with generations of *court-bouillon* to feel an instant affinity with the people who used it before. When the household goods of the great cook Elizabeth David went for auction in 1992, a few wooden spoons in an earthenware jar sold for 300 pounds. A colander went for 320 pounds, and her ancient wooden kitchen table, where she wrote her books, like the elegantly simple *French Provincial Cooking*, fetched 1,100 pounds.

"But it was nothing but battered pots and pans!" said an incredulous friend of the sale, "and a few sticks of pine furniture. Not even oak!" I didn't try to explain. I'm not sure I understood it myself.

To serve the potatoes, I'd chosen one of my own kitchen treasures, a deep, oval platter with a surface so irregular that it was clearly moulded by hand. Long before I acquired it, bakings by the hundred had glazed the exterior a glossy black, while the interior had modulated into the greeny yellow of old bronze. A short crack in one edge merely added to its allure, though it had counted sufficiently with the *brocanteuse* to say, "Oh, it's broken—so, say, a euro?" It would have been a bargain at fifty.

A dish for Pascal posed more problems. There simply wasn't one large enough, and I shrank from carving him in the kitchen and serving him in slices. Had we been in Paris, I might have borrowed one from an obliging restaurateur. They were still used by a few restaurants and big hotels that followed the tradition of displaying the dishes of the evening to guests as they enjoyed an aperitif in the bar. Waiters would carry in a side of lamb, a piglet, even a giant lobster, feelers weaving feebly, and parade it around the room before exiting to the kitchen. I'd been in one Irish restaurant where, as a whole gleaming salmon disappeared out the door, a guest who'd downed one cocktail too many yelled, "Hey, if nobody else wants it, I'll have it!"

A century ago, such dishes had been common. According to legend, Parisian courtesan Cora Pearl presented herself nude at a banquet for her admirers on such a dish, with a judiciously placed spray of parsley, and, some say, a delicate pink sauce. As late as 1959, surrealist artist Meret Oppenheim climaxed a feast by serving a nude girl on such a platter. More recently still, rock star Freddie Mercury, lead singer of Queen, titillated guests at his very gay parties by offering a nude boy squirming in a dish of raw liver.

Lacking the resources of Cora or Meret or Freddie, I was forced to improvise. From the same back room at the top of the house where the table leaf reposed between festivities, I unearthed a slab of cork bark almost a metre long. Peeled whole from the tree, it was apparently a long-forgotten souvenir of some long-ago Provençal holiday. Scoured of decades of dust and cobwebs, and lined with multiple layers of aluminium foil, it made a natural dish.

When I showed it to my mother-in-law, she blinked.

"Goodness," she said. "I'd forgotten I had that."

I was sufficiently superstitious to believe that it hadn't really been forgotten at all. It had just been waiting.

26

à table!

Soup's on!

—TRADITIONAL CALL TO EAT

And now the guests were starting to gather.

Too busy to take much notice, I shook their hands as each was ushered into the kitchen, then whisked out before they could do much damage.

About half had figured in our lives at some time or other, either from asking a favour or granting one. In France, your first recourse when you need something isn't to the Yellow Pages of the telephone directory but to your list of family and friends. A cousin had found a priest to marry us and christen Louise. Others recommended plumbers, carpenters, lawyers, and undertakers, pulled strings to speed visa applications, "fixed" banking problems, while we, in turn, did the same, as well as advising on the disposal of rare books and satisfying the curiosity of cousins who wanted to become writers or enter the film business. Anyone who wanted something written or read in English also came to me, so I found myself advising a pretty young relative applying for a job in America that saying she was "broad-minded and ready for anything" probably didn't convey the message she intended.

Some of the guests tonight had been at that first dinner so long ago. I couldn't mistake, for instance, the Falstaffian figure of my cousin by marriage Pierre-Michel, who was always trying to recruit us in dubious investment deals involving Luxembourg banks.

Then there was Jean-Paul, my adoptive uncle, whose acceptance of my anecdote about George Johnston's boozy tour of France had signalled acceptance into the clan. Now in his late eighties, he was descending into the physical and mental wilderness of senility. The neat blue suit of that first dinner had given way to a baggy sweater, crumpled corduroy trousers, and bedroom slippers. His wife, Françoise, manoeuvred him into his rightful seat at the head of the table, from which he looked around with the contentment of someone who lived in the perpetual present, with no memories to haunt him and no fears of what the future held. Ironi-

LE DERNIER USAGE
DE LA CIVILITÉ
POUR LA TABLE

cally, he probably saw me now as he had at that first dinner. I recognised the politely puzzled smile and the raised eyebrows that signalled, as they had then, "Who the hell is this?"

As for the rest, the family of my brother-in-law, Jean-Marie, was easy to spot: they were all huge. Anyone standing a head taller than the rest had to be a Glenisson. My own family, the Montels, were mostly distinguished by a prominent nose. The plump lady with the aristocratic beak, who'd embraced me so warmly, had to be Martine, my cousin by marriage. This was confirmed when she was joined by someone I knew better than any of them—her husband, Philippe, who, in middle age, had courageously abandoned his practice as a doctor to enter the church as a deacon. We'd attended his induction in Notre-Dame, held after hours, when the cathedral was closed to the public. In all that enormous space, there were just the twenty new deacons in their purple robes, the bishop and priests in charge of the ritual, and a few dozen invited guests. Its vast and cavernous dark engulfed us, a reminder, if one were needed, that the Church in France still retained its ancient ability to subdue and overawe.

My experience of most of my relations had been amiable. I would have been happier without the presence of a prune-faced cousin named Natalie and her cowed husband, Aristide, who trailed her like a poodle. But I looked for, and was happy not to find, the black sheep of the clan, like Nicolas, the schizophrenic cousin who threw his furniture out the window, and Simon, who invariably got drunk and groped the girls.

Marie-Do looked around the kitchen door.

"Can we start?"

I surveyed the state of dinner like a general surveying his forces before he issued the command "Charge!" Over the years, one develops a sense of timing, which ensures that everything arrives at the table at just the right state of cooking. I did a quick review.

Pascal? Crackling was forming satisfactorily, and a fork stuck deep into his haunch showed juices running clear, indicating that he was cooked right to the bone. Time, in fact, to remove him from the oven and let him "rest." Ten or fifteen minutes cooling would draw those juices back into the fibres, tenderising and lubricating the meat.

Potatoes? Golden and crusty on the outside, which meant, I knew, that their interiors were perfectly cooked. Time to take them out and arrange them on my precious earthenware platter.

Carrot pudding? Slightly risen in the dish, its coppery surface was pricked with points of deep brown where the sugar had caramelised. That too could come out of the oven and be allowed to cool. If anything, the flavour would improve.

"Yes. Serve the oysters."

This still left me at least ten minutes before I needed to sit down for the first course. Places had to be chosen, and the ritual observed, as far as possible, of alternating men and women, and, ideally, not letting couples sit together. There would be people who didn't want to be too close to the fire, and others who claimed to feel a draught. People had to be separated from their aperitif glasses—which reminded me that my own glass of *pineau* still sat, undrunk, on the kitchen counter. I hastily downed it, remembering my first cautious sip eighteen years before.

I lifted out the baking pan and examined the deep fat. There was no smell of burning, no black specks in the clear golden liquid, meaning I'd judged the oven temperature well, and the fat, once filtered, cooled, and congealed, could be used for many meals to come. Smeared on any cut of meat before roasting, it would provide better lubrication than those slices of raw lard preferred by French butchers. Potatoes, parsnips, and pumpkin would take on added flavour if roasted in it. It was ideal for preserving pork crackling or the liver and innards of a chicken, which the French call *gésiers*, and which add variety to a winter salad. And mixing it with shredded spiced pork created the delicious spread known as *rillettes*.

A preoccupation with cholesterol had made beef and pork fat politically unacceptable almost everywhere, but the French still respected the savour of good pork or beef fat, and I was proud to go along with them.

"Dripping", as it used to be called, had been a venerable and valuable element of the Anglo-Saxon diet for millennia. Pancake batter poured into bubbling hot fat puffed up and browned into Yorkshire pudding, absorbing the flavours of the meat and helping it go further. Spread on bread, it became "bread and dripping", a favourite snack of the prewar British working class. Dripping was an invaluable ingredient of the best pastry, the crispest French fries. During World War II, under a programme called Fat for Britain, we more fortunate colonials were even asked to save our dripping and send it in jars to our deprived cousins in Britain. (We assumed they were grateful, though it's not something every person would be glad to receive in the mail.)

Pouring off the fat from Pascal's cooking left a molasses-thick residue of reduced juices in the pan. Placing it on a low flame, I waited for it to bubble, then splashed in another bottle of Guinness. What had been an unappetising sludge thinned to the consistency of varnish, then, with more stout, to an unctuous sauce of deep bronze, slick with fat, fragrant with the spices of the marinade. I tasted it, added a pinch of *fleur de sel*, and lowered the heat to drive off the last of the alcohol and dissolve any fragments of congealed juices that remained.

Had I been wearing a chef's toque and *tablier*, I could have removed them now. The dinner was all but complete. All that remained was the carving, the serving—mechanical work that could be done by anyone.

Instead, I washed my hands and face at the sink, took a deep breath, and left the kitchen behind. Between one door and the next, I crossed the most crucial frontier in the world of food. I stepped through the kitchen door a cook—I entered the dining room an eater.

27

The Dinner

Show me another pleasure like dinner
which comes every day and lasts an hour.
—CHARLES MAURICE DE TALLEYRAND

Through hundreds of dinner parties, I've striven to find a metaphor that describes their special fascination.

An invasion? Yes, in the sense that one must overcome the resistance of some people to dishes they don't know, or don't like, or to the people they're forced to sit next to and to engage in often aimless conversation.

A seduction? That too—as demonstrated in Isak Dinesen's story *Babette's Feast*, and Gabriel Axel's film, where a French female chef, exiled to a remote Scandinavian religious community, repays them by cooking a sumptuous dinner. Initially, the richness of the food—

turtle soup, quail served with caviar and cream in a sarcophagus of pastry—dismays her dour guests. Privately, they decide that, though they must eat so as not to hurt her feelings, they will resist enjoying it. But they underestimate her art, and before the last course they are transformed.

A ritual? That most of all. There was enough religion in me to see all meals as sacramental, and this one especially. Religion was full of food: bread and wine, fish and fowl, flesh and blood. When Christ felt his time on earth was coming to an end, he summoned his disciples not to a sermon but to a supper.

Serving six oysters to each of eighteen people is a logistical challenge, a juggling act involving wedges of lemon, the correct miniature forks, the circulation of sliced baguette, and the acceptance of praise for the succulence and freshness of M. Papin's product.

Or otherwise.

It was Marie-Do's cousin Natalie—there's one in every crowd—who raised a polite complaint that we hadn't provided a dish of the detestable vinegar-and-shallot sauce. I feigned momentary deafness, and Marie-Do changed the subject by informing the table at large, "When we were in Australia, we had oysters quite often.

But it's incredible—the Australians remove them from the shell and *wash* them before putting them back."

There was a moment of appalled silence. Sluice out the delicious juices? The essence of the ocean that gives the oyster its special savor? You might as well deprive a nightingale of its song or a beautiful woman of her hair.

"Unbelievable!"

"A barbarism!"

"What a country!"

In the collective astonishment, the question of vinegar and onions was forgotten.

As the emptied shells were gathered up, the bowls of sliced baguette replenished, glasses refilled, I ducked into the kitchen for the last few tasks of the meal.

The roll of stuffing separated cleanly from the well-greased foil. I sliced it into rounds and arranged them, moistened with a little of the gravy, on a large platter with the carrot pudding at the centre.

The potatoes, rounded down by initial boiling, had become crisp golden cannonballs of carbohydrate. Piled in my precious dish, they could have made a perfect illustration in any cookbook.

Last of the side dishes was the apple compote. Baked slowly at the bottom of the oven in a covered dish with nothing more than a knob of salted butter, the Clochards had subsided into caramelised tenderness. Sweetness and tartness, salt and fragrance, combined in this best of all accompaniments.

As it was placed on the table, my brother-in-law, Jean-Marie, bent over the dish of sliced stuffing and carrot pudding, as if examining a new and puzzling creature found under an overturned rock. His grunt indicated a provisional acceptance.

In the kitchen, careful not to shatter the shell of bubbled deep brown crackling into which his skin had been transformed, I transferred Pascal from the board to my improvised dish of cork bark. Eyes closed, fore-feet together, back legs curled under him, he appeared to bear no ill will for the way we had shortened his already brief life. An apple in his mouth would have been an in-dignity. Better to preserve his expression of resignation, even complacency.

And surely he would have been pleased at the roar of approval that greeted his ritual circumnavigation of the table before he was installed in the place of honour. It had been a short life, if not a merry one, but it would conclude by giving pleasure to others—a not ignoble end.

All seemed to be going well. Taking my place at the foot of the table, I gathered up the carving knife and fork and prepared to peel off the crackling before I cut into the succulent meat.

But then Cousin Natalie sniffed suspiciously.

"What's that funny smell?"

"... erm, yes," echoed Aristide. He cleared his throat. "Funny ... er ... smell."

"Just a little spice," I said.

"Spice?" The corners of Natalie's mouth turned down. "Oh, I don't know if I would care for ..."

"No," said Aristide. "Don't care for ..." He laid a pale, moist strangler's hand on his ample stomach. "... Digestion ..."

But Marie-Do was prepared. Better than anyone, she knew how to deal with people like these.

"Ah, but this is what they call Cajun cooking—which means, of course, 'Acadian'."

Natalie looked blank. Fortunately, my sister-in-law, Caroline, is an expert on the French colonisation of North America, and the author of several books on the subject.

In 1755, she explained, the British ejected five thousand French settlers from Canada. Many headed south, to join the French community in Louisiana started by the whores forcibly deported to the new colony to provide wives for the colonists. The new arrivals combined the tradition of French food with the exotic ingredients and spices of their new home to create a unique cuisine. Since they kept their original Canadian name—"Acadian"— they, and their food, became known as Cajun.

"And do you know," she continued, "the Jesuits who went to Canada with the first settlers wrote out songs for the Indians, which have been lost or forgotten in France itself. Canadian archives actually contain pieces of music that we don't even possess in France."

"So . . ." asked Françoise pointedly, "it's really *French*?"

"Oh, completely," said Caroline.

I picked up the carving knife and fork and cut into Pascal with a delicious crunch of crackling.

"Who wants the first slice?"

". . . erm . . ." With a nervous glance at Natalie, Aristide held out his plate.

It would be nice to tell you that I recall every instant of the meal that followed. Nothing would give me greater pleasure than to go over the reaction to each dish: the looks of appreciation, the frowns of doubt, the toasts and bons mots, the portions left half-eaten and the plates wiped clean . . .

But anyone who has ever served a big meal knows it isn't like that.

Mostly, you're too busy to eat, let alone watch. Bowls and dishes have to be ferried to and from the table, plates filled and passed, sauce boats replenished, extra bread brought, dishes explained, recipes summarised—not to mention arguments adjudicated, reminiscences patiently listened to, glances exchanged, eyebrows raised ... all the choreography of a social event that no menu can possibly reflect. Every meal is a world of its own, from which we emerge, however subtly, changed.

It took the best part of forty minutes to dispose of Pascal, but when we began clearing the table for dessert, nothing remained except a pile of bones. Even the snout and tail had been eaten—probably by Aristide, who, with the help of half a dozen glasses of Bordeaux, had asserted himself furiously. Tucking his napkin into his collar, he'd launched himself at his dinner as if he wouldn't get another for a week—which, from Natalie's disapproving glares, was probably the case. But even she picked fastidiously at a slice and came back for more. Pascal had not died in vain.

Now it was time to see how they liked my dessert.

I took the wide flat ceramic dish out of the refrigerator and carried it to the table, draped in a fresh linen tea towel. Conversation halted as I laid it in the place formerly occupied by Pascal and lifted the cloth.

The Dinner

What they saw was some sort of fruit salad, covered in a layer of . . . what? Something brown, granular . . .

One could sense the feeling of disappointment. There was a general air of anticlimax—until I produced the butane torch.

"Stand back!"

I flicked the trigger. A jet of blue flame leaped out.

One of the young cousins squealed. Someone else swore; I didn't see who because I was preoccupied with playing the roaring flame over the surface of the dessert. As I did so, the crushed palm sugar laid across the mixture of tropical fruit and mascarpone cheese melted into a translucent golden glaze.

Once all the sugar had liquified, I turned off the torch, waited a few seconds, then tapped the surface with a spoon. It gave back a reassuring *tok tok*.

"Fruits brûlés?" I asked.

The table erupted in applause.

28

Washing Up

'Tis the gift to be simple,
'Tis the gift to be free,
'Tis the gift to come down
Where we ought to be,
And when we find ourselves in the place just right,
'Twill be in the valley of love and delight.

—OLD SHAKER HYMN

To the victor, they say, go the spoils.

But to the victor of a big meal, unfortunately, goes the washing-up.

Of course, everyone tries to help. But a small kitchen can hold only so many people, and by the time you've explained that *those* plates don't go in the dishwasher and *that* dish should be put in the fridge, it's easier to do it yourself.

Also, a heavy meal takes its toll. Eating that much food, not to mention drinking so much wine, leaves a person *relaxed*. From the front bedrooms, thunderous snores soon indicated that at least two of the male guests were sleeping it off. The occasional creak and soft footfall from above my head suggested that one of the younger cousins and her boyfriend had discovered that narrow bed in the back room and were enjoying what the French call a *sieste crapuleuse*.

Almost everyone else had gone next door to the home of Françoise and Jean-Paul, the adults to gossip, the kids to watch TV.

Which left me to clean up.

Well, I didn't mind, to tell the truth. It was a chance to unwind, to relive the high points of the meal, and of this Christmas.

I walked to the glass doors of the big dining room and looked out at the garden that fell away to the distant hedge marking the end of the family's property.

The land meant a great deal to me now, since I'd become part of it—or it of me.

In earlier centuries, this had been a farm. During World War II, under the German occupation—if a *feldwebel* and two enlisted men billeted in the village really counted as "occupation"—it had become a kitchen garden, planted with beans, cabbage, and potatoes to feed the family. Forty years later, Marie-Do and I held our wedding reception there, and a few years later, we'd watched Louise and her cousins scamper on Easter morning, searching for eggs scattered by the bells returning from Rome.

My mother-in-law had inherited this land from her parents, as Marie-Dominique and Caroline would inherit it in time, then Alice and Louise, continuing a line unbroken for half a millennium. In this country, one didn't possess land or houses, any more than you possessed a river. They owned you, and sooner or later, whether you liked it or not, they would coax you into the stream as they had coaxed me, involving you in their eddies and cataracts, carrying you on to the open sea.

How many other travellers had been welcomed into such families over the centuries? People like myself were the vagabonds of the world, distant descendants of the fugitive and dispossessed, the beggar monks, troubadours, scholars, and chronically footloose voyagers for whom generations of more settled householders had baked cakes, hiding a coin inside as a discreet gift to help them on their way. We came to the door at midnight, to be offered food, drink, money, and, if we were fortunate, the love of someone within that family, and the security and comfort of its table and hearth.

Not to be cast out, no longer to be a poor man and a stranger—what gift could be greater than that?

Appendix 1

Recipes

Cajun/Indian Dry-Rubbed Roast Pork

Ingredients.

A sucking piglet of about 16 lb. (A pig of this size serves about 18 people. The marinade can be reduced proportionately for a leg or shoulder, or a rack of chops. In every case, the meat must retain its skin.)

For the marinade.

3 or 4 cloves of garlic, peeled.

1 tsp cardamon seeds or powdered cardamon.

2 or 3 large dried chillis, depending on size and taste, including seeds.

1 tbsp dried paprika, smoked for preference.

10 peppercorns.

1 tsp sugar.

1 tbsp dry mustard.

1 tsp salt.

Olive oil.

2 or 3 pints Guinness stout.

Method.

With a very sharp knife, score the skin of the pork in parallel cuts about ½ inch apart, making sure you cut down to the underlying layer of fat but not into the meat.

Place the spices in a blender or mortar, and grind or pound until fine. Crush the garlic into the spice mix, and add enough oil to create a thick paste. Rub the paste into the meat, working it into the spaces between the cuts and, if using a whole pig, into the interior. Wrap the piglet well in shrinkwrap or foil, or a well-sealed plastic bag, and place in the refrigerator for at least 24 hours.

An hour before cooking, remove the piglet or joint from the refrigerator and unwrap. If using a piglet, stuff the cavity and sew up with twine. Otherwise, form the stuffing into a loaf or cylinder and wrap in well-buttered foil.

Pre-heat the oven to 350 degrees. Place the piglet on an oven rack with a deep pan below to catch drippings. Cook for 20 minutes per pound, i.e. about 5 hours. (Internal temperature should be 155 to 160 degrees.) Every hour, turn the piglet, basting it with its drippings, then with Guinness.

If serving roast potatoes, place them in the drippings

about an hour before the pig is cooked. At the same time, if the stuffing is being cooked separately, place low in the oven. Also the compote.

Remove the pig from the oven and allow it to rest for about 30 minutes before carving.

Allow the drippings to settle, then drain off the fat. Deglaze the pan with Guinness, cook off the alcohol and reduce the sauce to the preferred consistency. Correct the seasoning.

The piglet can be carved at the table, but it's often easier to display it to the guests, then return to the kitchen for carving. Remove the crackling and divide into portions. Slice the stuffing, or place it in a bowl. Carve the pork and serve on a warmed dish, passing round the sauce and compote.

For the stuffing.

1 large onion.
4 sticks of celery, with leaves.
1 clove garlic.
1 egg.
1 apple.
6 cups soft white breadcrumbs.
1 tbsp dried sage, crumbled, or 6 fresh sage leaves.
Salt and ground black pepper.

Method.

Peel and chop the onion. Peel, quarter and chop the apple, roughly chop the celery, including leaves. Place all ingredients in a food processor and blend. (The mixture should be dry and crumbly. The apple and celery will break down in cooking, providing any necessary moisture.)

For the apple compote.

8 apples, ideally Clochard or Chanticleer, but, if not available, Granny Smiths.

1 tbsp salted butter.

White pepper.

Method.

Peel and core the apples, and cut into eighths. Arrange them in a heavy-bottomed dish with the butter and pepper. Cover and place in the oven about an hour before serving. Check occasionally to see that the apples are not burning; this will depend on the amount of sugar in them. Ideally, they should be tender rather than mushy, and slightly caramelised.

Carrot Pudding

Ingredients.

2 lb carrots
1 egg.
1 cup cream cheese.
1 tsp ground cumin.
¼ tsp turmeric.
¼ tsp cayenne or chilli powder (if liked).
¼ tsp ground coriander.
Knob of butter.

Method.

Peel the carrots and steam until tender. Allow to cool, then place in a food processor with the other ingredients and process until smooth. Add salt and freshly ground pepper to taste. Place in a shallow dish, pattern the surface with a fork to create ridges, and bake in a medium oven for 30 minutes or until high points show some browning.

Baked Potatoes

Ingredients.

2 lb large, old potatoes (new potatoes of whatever size don't lend themselves to roasting)

1 lb butter, beef or goose dripping, or other animal fat. (Don't substitute oil, or the potatoes will be leathery.)

Method.

Peel the potatoes and halve or quarter them into chunks of roughly equal size. Place in cold water until needed. An hour before serving, steam or parboil them in salted water for about 7 minutes. They should be tender to a knife point for the first ¼ inch but still hard at the centre. Drain well. If cooking under a roast, place them in the pan, avoiding spatter from the water used in cooking. Otherwise, heat the butter or dripping until near smoking, then drop potatoes in one by one. They should be half immersed but not floating. Cook for about 20 minutes, turning frequently. Remove when evenly browned, and drain on absorbent paper.

Christmas Pudding

Puddings should be made well ahead of time; at least a month, though it's possible to store them, under the right conditions, for more than a year.

Ingredients.

(makes two puddings, each for four persons)

1 lb unsalted butter.

2 cups raisins.

1 cup candied peel, finely sliced.

2 cups brandy.

2 cups white breadcrumbs.

1 cup ground almonds.

¼ cup soft brown sugar.

3 tbsp flour.

¼ tsp finely grated lemon zest.

¼ tsp finely grated orange zest.

Pinch ground cinnamon.

Pinch freshly grated nutmeg.

1 egg.

½ tsp dark treacle, molasses or golden syrup.

½ cup Guinness.

2 tbsp fresh orange juice.

1 tsp fresh lemon juice.

Method.

Soak the raisins in the brandy for an hour. Drain, reserving the brandy. In a large bowl, mix the raisins, candied fruits, softened butter, breadcrumbs, almonds, sugar, flour, zests, cinnamon, and nutmeg, using your hands if necessary to achieve an even and unctuous mix. Combine the egg and treacle/molasses/golden syrup in another bowl. Stir in the beer, juices, and brandy, add to fruit mixture, and mix into a gluey batter.

Puddings may be cooked in bowls or cloths.

If using cloths, boil two large cotton or linen squares, e.g. tea towels, allow to dry, sprinkle liberally with flour, and divide the batter between them. Gather each into sack form and tie tightly at the neck with twine.

If using bowls, butter two ceramic or glass bowls, divide the batter between them, cover each bowl with two layers of waxed paper, then foil, and secure with twine.

To cook, place the puddings, whether in cloths or bowls, over boiling water in a large pot, cover, and steam for about 5 hours, topping up the water as needed.

Remove the puddings, allow them to cool, and store in a cool, dry place, or refrigerator. To reheat, steam for an hour, then turn out onto dish.

Traditionally, Christmas pudding is presented at the table doused in flaming brandy, and served with custard, ice cream and/or brandy butter, sometimes called hard sauce.

Brandy Butter, or Hard Sauce

Ingredients.

½ cup soft butter.
½ cups sifted icing sugar.
2 tbsp brandy.

Method.

Process all ingredients until blended. Form into a roll on foil, chill, and slice into small discs for serving.

Mary-Over-the-Road's Italian Potato Salad

Ingredients.

1 lb waxy potatoes, e.g. Rosenval Reds.
1 red onion.
Olive oil.
Dried herbs – oregano, sage, or *herbes de Provence*.
Ground black pepper

Method.

Peel the potatoes, boil and allow to cool. While they are still lukewarm, cut them into thick slices or chunks, and mix with thin rings of onion. Drizzle with olive oil, salt, freshly ground pepper, and dried herbs. Toss lightly and serve lukewarm or at room temperature. If you need to refrigerate this dish overnight, allow it to reach room temperature again before re-serving, and refresh with a splash of olive oil. This is a good dish to show off an exceptionally fruity or fragrant oil.

Marie-Dominique's Vinaigrette Superieur

Ingredients.

(enough for a green salad for four, or a dish of lukewarm steamed vegetables, e.g. asparagus or leeks.)

Olive oil.
Cider vinegar.
1 egg yolk.
French mustard.
Honey.
Pinch salt

Method.

In a small bowl, use a hand whisk to blend a teaspoon of mustard with a teaspoon of honey. Add the raw egg yolk, a pinch of salt and about a tablespoon of vinegar. Whisk together while trickling in some olive oil. Continue to whisk until the ingredients achieve liaison, and the dressing becomes golden and creamy. Test the seasoning by dipping in a finger and licking (also works if the finger belongs to someone else). Leftover dressing keeps well in a jar in the refrigerator. If it separates, a brisk shake restores homogeneity.

Pork Chops with Calvados and Apples

This dish works best with thick chops that retain their fat. Thinly cut chops dry out. It also works well with veal chops. Slow cooking is the essence of the dish, which will burn at anything but the lowest heat. If your stove top is too hot, cook it in a medium oven.

Ingredients.

1 thick pork or veal chop per person.

Apples, ideally Clochard or Chanticleer, but Granny Smiths at a pinch, in the proportion of half an apple to each chop.

Calvados apple brandy.

Unsalted butter.

Salt and ground black pepper

Method.

Peel and core the apples and cut into eighths. Heat a generous quantity of butter in a wide, shallow pan with a lid, and sauté the chops until sealed on both sides and just beginning to brown.

Place the pieces of apple around the chops in the pan, cover, and reduce the heat to the minimum. Cook, covered, for 20 minutes, not lifting the lid unless the butter appears to be burning.

At the end of that time, the meat should be tender, and the apples partly caramelised. Transfer the chops and apples to a serving dish. Pour off any excess fat in the pan and deglaze with Calvados. Allow the alcohol to cook off, season with salt and pepper, and pour the sauce over the meat.

Appendix 2

A Parisian Christmas: the ten commandments

If you're invited to a French home for Christmas, take it as more than a compliment. It signifies you are almost a member of the family. But before you accept, think about the following.

1. Are you sure your French is up to it? Few French people speak English, and even they prefer not to do so on family occasions. You risk being seated with an elderly gentleman who demands your opinion of Clemenceau's policy on the *entente cordiale*.

2. Conversation is a minefield. Subjects shunned in the Anglo world, like politics, religion and money, are embraced; but never ask a French person what he or she does for a living. Inquire of a man about his children or his car, and compliment a woman on her dress; nobody has such an eagle eye for labels as a *française*.

3. At Christmas, as on any other occasion, never bring food or drink. To arrive with a bottle of wine implies you didn't think your host would provide any. As for a cake or cheese, proffering these may be construed as a mortal insult. (Imagine turning up at an English house with your own knife, fork and plate.)

4. If you feel you must offer something, choose a neutral item—chocolates, flowers, or some item for the house. But it's far safer to come empty-handed. It implies that your presence is the greatest gift—a very French attitude.

5. No matter how close the relationship, avoid any gift that might be thought intimate. This includes clothes, particularly robes, pyjamas, nightgowns, and, naturally, lingerie. Also items relating to the body: lotions, creams, perfumes, and soaps. ("You think we smell bad, *M'sieur?*") When I suggested offering a Waterpik toothbrush to my mother-in-law, my daughter blanched. "It would be like giving her . . ." She groped for some sufficiently horrible comparison. ". . . toilet paper!"

6. Don't offer to assist in the kitchen—help the host carve, or distribute the plates. Above all, do not propose toasts: to the cook, your hosts, the French Republic, An-

glo-French friendship or the immortal memory of Jim Morrison. As outsiders, you are guests of honour. It's more likely your host will toast you. If he does, a responding toast isn't expected. A simple *"merci"* will suffice.

7. If you're vegetarian, vegan, or allergic to anything edible, you shouldn't be at a French table. Having accepted, however, you must eat what's put in front of you, or at least toy with it. To refuse is to reject the most important element of the invitation—hospitality. Likewise, if something is particularly delicious, don't ask for the recipe. It probably came from a *traiteur* or Picard, the gourmet frozen-food chain, and the hostess just added a sprig of parsley.

8. Diplomats traditionally leave after the second cup of coffee. Wait an hour, then suggest you should be on your way. You'll soon gauge whether your hosts want you to stay. Mostly they won't. Christmas, like Thanksgiving in America, is a time for thrashing out family matters and catching up with relatives seen only once a year—not things one does in front of strangers.

9. Never invite French people to Christmas dinner. Chances are they're expected at the home of their

parents, or an aunt from whom they hope to inherit a château. Your invitation will interrupt their plans, and arouse only resentment. Also, not knowing Anglo-etiquette, they will spend the meal worrying about how to behave, and hate you for ever. Send them a nice card instead.

10. That said, few French people bother with Christmas cards. If they do, the correct time to send and receive them is not before Christmas but around New Year, and they continue to arrive right up to Twelfth Night. On consideration, it's safer to meet them for a drink in mid-January.

In fact, maybe that's what you should do, rather than accept that invitation to Christmas dinner in the first place . . .

Rudy Gelenter

ABOUT THE AUTHOR

John Baxter is an Australian-born writer, journalist and film-maker. Baxter has lived in Britain and the United States as well as his native Sydney, but has made his home in Paris since 1989. He is married to the film-maker Marie-Dominique Montel, and they have one daughter, Louise.